Evangelisation in England & Wales

a report to the Catholic bishops

Philip Knights & Andrea Murray
Foreword by Bishop Crispian Hollis

Catholic Bishops' Conference of England & Wales

Evangelisation in England and Wales: a report to the Catholic bishops
by Philip Knights and Andrea Murray

Copyright © 2002 Catholic Bishops' Conference of England and Wales

www.catholic-ew.org.uk

Published by the Catholic Communications Service,
39 Eccleston Square, London SW1V 1BX. ccs@cbcew.org.uk

Designed by Tom Horwood
Printed by MPG Books Ltd, Bodmin, Cornwall

ISBN 0 905241 24 X

Contents

Foreword

There seems to be a 'conspiracy' of events which make this report particularly welcome at this moment.

Cardinal Murphy-O'Connor is making evangelisation a major feature of the many talks and addresses that he is giving, beginning with his challenging words to the National Conference of Priests last year.

This year's CTBI Forum took as its theme, 'In Search of Holy Ground', which challenged the participants, drawn from all the Churches of Great Britain and Ireland, to identify and proclaim the presence of Christ in our world.

A recent gathering of bishops and young people throughout Europe again concentrated on evangelisation as a major theme.

Our own bishops of England and Wales are taking evangelisation as the major topic for their autumn 2002 Study Week in Guernsey, and this work by Dr Philip Knights and Andrea Murray is essential background reading for that. It helps us immeasurably to know where we are and what is already being achieved - or not achieved, as the case may be. It represents that necessary research which has to be at the heart of any worthwhile study of the way in which the people of God hold their faith and are challenged to share it with others.

It will provide seminal material for the forthcoming work of the newly formed Agency for Evangelisation.

I welcome this work most warmly, as did all the bishops of England and Wales at their Low Week 2002 meeting. It gives us the understanding and the detail of the context in which we have to respond to the urgent call that the Lord puts before all his disciples 'to go out and proclaim the Good News'.

+Crispian Hollis

The Rt Rev Crispian Hollis
Bishop of Portsmouth
Chairman, Department of Mission and Unity,
Catholic Bishops' Conference of England and Wales

1. Introduction to the project

This report is the fruit of research into evangelisation[1] in England and Wales commissioned by the Interim Management Committee of the proposed Agency for Evangelisation (IMC) with a brief to report to the Bishops' Conference. Funding has come from the Bishops' Conference, the Catholic Missionary Society and the Board of Vocations.

The two researchers have been The Rev Dr Philip Knights CMS and Mrs Andrea Murray. Dr Knights is based at the CMS Mission House in North London, Mrs Murray at Ushaw College.

Our remit has been:

- To consider the principles of mission and evangelisation at the beginning of the twenty-first century.
- To review current practice.
- To make recommendations for the future development of evangelisation in England and Wales.

In all these areas the Catholic Church in England and Wales has been the focus. However, due notice has been given to initiatives elsewhere in the world and to the practice of our ecumenical partners.

Research methodology

There have been four strands of research:

1. The collation of theological and other background material. This has drawn on a large number of Church documents and statements, resources, conferences, reports and other publications.

2. A questionnaire sent out to several constituencies which concentrated on the experience of evangelisation as experienced

---

[1] We shall prefer the English spelling but for purposes of accuracy many quotations will retain their American (international) spelling of *evangelization*.

by those active inside the Church, i.e. those who have been evangelised. We were aware that this was skewed to be a sample of 'Core' and 'Super-Core' Catholics.

3. This has been broadened by interviews with practitioners and participation observation in a significant variety of evangelisation activities, initiatives and agencies.

4. The findings of these are being examined through a series of conversations with representatives of a number of lenses, such as school, family, Justice and Peace, New Movements, women and vocations.

While these layers of research have in some senses been sequential, they have also been interlinked and have informed each other. Thus we began with some theological and to some extent theoretical principles which provided a starting point for the survey. With this basis we approached agencies and initiatives. The experience of preparing the survey, meeting practitioners and gaining responses has led us to refine our theological reflections through the forge of experience and practice.

The questionnaires went through several drafts, and pilot surveys were made in a variety of circumstances. This consultation enabled us to focus more clearly on issues and to work through some ambiguities of language. Four sets of questions were prepared: General Survey (the largest with over 1,100 respondents); Survey of Parish Priests; Survey of Bishops and Diocesan Workers; Survey of Seminarians. The questionnaires all had the same basic structure, although presented in ways appropriate to the various constituencies. Some more technical questions were addressed to professional workers.

Each survey looked at the personal experience and faith of respondents, the Christian community of the respondent, the respondent's personal experience of mission and evangelisation, and mission and evangelisation in the respondent's community. Within these areas we investigated the background demographics of the sample; the importance of faith in the respondent's life; the vitality of parish life; how faith and life connected; how proclamation, community and service were experienced; what had ignited a sense of the Gospel in people's life; and their awareness of and understanding of mission and evangelisation in their personal and communal life.

More information on the surveys themselves, proportionate responses and the statistical confidence of each survey are presented in the Appendix to this report. Chapter 6 presents a digest of data and analysis of statistics gained from this survey. However, responses from the survey have informed each section of this report. Some responses from the surveys and other interviews have been included as boxes within the text of the Report.

We sought to visit a wide range, and hopefully representative sample, of practitioners. In meeting with individuals, communities, groups and agencies, we interviewed them about their practice and where possible observed them at work. We are very grateful to the hospitality we received and the generosity and openness with which we were met. Rooting our thinking in the actual experience of evangelisation initiatives has been invaluable.

We were also aware of a number of consultative bodies and interested groups in the Church. We have tried to present our chief findings to representatives from many areas. These have both enabled us to clarify priorities and check that our findings corresponded to their experiences. Their insights have been very helpful in formulating the analysis of our research findings.

Reporting

There have been several moments of reporting. The primary body to whom we were asked to report has been the Bishops' Conference of England and Wales itself. The work has been reported through the Interim Management Committee of the proposed Agency for Evangelisation and also to the Department of Mission and Unity of the Bishops' Conference, and within this to the Home Mission Committee. A sub-committee of these (with some co-opted members) acted as a management and support group with whom the researchers were in frequent consultation. The Bishops' Conference has decided that there should be a wider publication of the major findings of the research. Further details of the research as well as statistics collated can be found on the internet at {www.cms.org.uk/research}.

2. Theological background and other issues

What is evangelisation?

Evangelisation is the origin, purpose and destiny of the Church. The Christian community is here because of the Gospel. We exist to proclaim and enact the Good News of Jesus and to see the fulfilment of that Gospel in the kingdom of God. In the midst of some ambiguity, the very first thing to be said about evangelisation is that it is neither something extra to be added to the work of hard pressed bishops, clergy, religious and laity, nor a specialised option for those who like that sort of thing; it is the work of the Church. There is an intimate connection between the Church and evangelisation: the Church is born out of the Gospel of Jesus, she is the community of the

Some responses to the question, *When you hear the word 'Evangelisation' what comes into mind?*

- bringing Christ to others
- hyper-activism
- do-gooders
- pressurising people
- Billy Graham
- not my type of music
- the word has a bad name
- form of 'showing off'
- spreading the word of God
- enthusiasm
- reimaging the Gospel
- 'happy clappy' won't let me worship in peace
- fear
- well-intentioned but too narrow minded

evangelised, she is the depository of the Good News and the home from which evangelisers are sent into the world.[2]

We therefore wish to celebrate the many things which the Church does and to understand them as acts which proclaim and enact the Good News of Jesus: that is to say, evangelisation. The Gospel is alive in our midst: the Gospel is the life of the Church. We thus primarily see evangelisation as a positive hermeneutic of the life of God's people expressed in personal conversion, ecclesial renewal and social transformation. All we are authentically as Christians needs to be understood from the perspective of the Gospel and thus from the perspective of evangelisation.

[2] Cf. Pope Paul VI, *Evangelii Nuntiandi* (1975) 15.

Nonetheless we must acknowledge that few terms are capable of such fluidity of meaning as *Mission, Evangelisation* or *Evangelism*.

The terminology: 'evangelization', 'evangelism', 'mission', 'witness' and so forth is slippery. Many different shades of meaning are given to these terms.[3]

One collector of mission statistics has found 79 definitions of evangelism and evangelisation, and this is no complete list.[4] Evangelisation has become an umbrella term to shelter within itself several concepts. For some evangelisation is the initial presentation of the Gospel to those who are not Christians, for others it is a synonym for the entirety of the Christian mission.[5] We will contend that evangelisation is wider than the former yet more specific than the latter.[6] In particular we will argue that there are specific elements which must be included within a comprehensive understanding of evangelisation.

[3] Aylward Shorter WF, *Evangelization and Culture* (Geoffrey Chapman, London, 1994), p. x.

[4] David Barratt quoted by David Bosch, *Transforming Mission: Paradigm Shifts in Theology of Mission* (Orbis, Maryknoll NY, 1991), p. 409.

[5] Cf. '"Evangelizzazione" è un termine chiave della missiologia e gode di un impiego così ovvio che non sempre si fa sufficientemente attenezione alla sua attuale ambiguatà. Da una parte può significare il primo annuncio del'Evangelo in un ambiente non ancora cristiano, dall'altra designa anche tutto il compito che la Chiesa svolge davanti al mondo; "evangelizzazione" diventa così quasi sinonimo di quell'altra nozione indespensibile nella teologia missionaria che è, appunto, la "missione" Anche questa parola non si rivela univoca, ma ci mette a confronto con diversi contenuti concettuali tra i quali spicca l'attività missionaria specificamente diretta ai non-battezzati, anche se può egualmente riferirsi al mandato globale della Chiesa che prolunga nella storia la missione de Cristo per la salvezza umana.' *Dizionario di Missiologia* (Pontifica Università Urbana, Edizioni Dehoniane, Bologna, 1993), p. 245.

[6] It is not that we shall resist the interrelatedness of concepts of evangelisation and mission, but that we shall present evangelisation as a frame within which to understand mission.

Evangelisation involves the enactment of the Gospel as well as (or indeed as part of) its proclamation. Evangelisation is something which must happen to the Church to enable the Church to evangelise. It is in hearing, accepting and living the Gospel that the Church can share it. We will also suggest that evangelisation, as a rich and complex process of proclaiming and living the Gospel, will necessitate distinct responses to distinct circumstances. It is not that evangelisation is in itself ambiguous and multivocal: it always remains the encounter of the Good News of God in Christ with people in the world participated in by the Church, and the consequent and inherent spread and establishment of the content and fruits of that Good News. However, the locations of that encounter will vary and the experience of that encounter will also vary. To those suffering from injustice and oppression evangelisation must involve the material transformation of society and release from those things which dehumanise and victimise them; for the sinner and the wounded evangelisation must involve news of forgiveness and healing; for the Church evangelisation must involve constant renewal in the Gospel. The integral liberation that comes in Christ touches all dimensions of humanity: evangelisation must therefore address all the dimensions of humanity.

There must be a distinction between evangelisation in the context of no previous contact with the Gospel and those contexts in which elements of the Gospel or seeds of the Gospel are present. We are aware that the grace of God is active in the world. We do not approach those who are unknown to God or to whom God has denied his love. We are following the love of God into God's world. The world and people within it are not a *tabula rasa* with no experience of the Spirit or insight into the Divine, but the location of a movement in God's love and pilgrims (even if unconsciously) in a context of divine grace. Thus one consequence of this is that dialogue and co-operation with men and women of good will in many fields (culture, arts, world religions, politics, community organisations, education etc.) has become far more prominent in understanding evangelisation today than was the case in previous generations. A further consequence is that when we consider evangelisation in England and Wales we are conscious that we are in a context calling for 'New Evangelisation'[7] - a position in which the Gospel has historically been proclaimed, and to some

> Evangelisation is connecting with individuals in the place where God is. *Representative of Women's Lens*

extent or to a varying degree been accepted, but which demands a new presentation so that there can be a new acceptance of the fullness of the Good News today. Our work is to both discover and build upon that of God which is already present.

We have been conscious of a wide variety of interpretations of evangelisation among our dialogue partners and survey respondents. We have therefore formulated this working definition:

> **Evangelisation is the proclamation and enactment of the Good News of Christ. This is an essential aspect of the mission of the Church. We are privileged to participate in God's purposes of love for his people and his world. The Church is obliged to share the Good News with all people. This sharing involves the penetration and integration of the Good News of Jesus into all dimensions of humanity. It thus encompasses: Christian witness; presentation of the Good News to those who have not heard it; initiation into the Church through catechesis; the ongoing formation of Christian believers and communities; the renewal of the Church; and all actions which further the building of God's Kingdom of love, justice and peace.**

In travelling over most of England and Wales in the course of this last year we have repeatedly encountered a companion which has stimulated an inchoate series of musings. The bushy *Buddleia davidii* has accompanied us from presbytery gardens to

---

[7] See below for more upon the use of 'New Evangelisation' in the teaching of John Paul II.

railway embankments, on waste ground, even on the roofs of factories. It is named after the extraordinary Basque Lazarist missionary Père Armand David.[8] This adventurous naturalist may be better known for the deer named after him but the omnipresent 'Butterfly Bush' and many other species of garden plants are also to be laid at his door.

The first layer of musings about evangelisation this inspired were therefore concerned with exploration and discovery and openness to the new. Such after all was the attitude of Père David. Partly this struck a chord because we were explorers seeking to discover what was there in the Catholic Church, but more because all evangelisation is an exploration to discover anew the love, grace and presence of God in and through the Church, in people's lives, and in God's world. Evangelisers today are exploring the present situation of people in England and Wales so that the Gospel of Jesus may be discovered as Good News for today. This involves an attitude of openness to what is there to be discovered and a willingness to go beyond the known and the safe. Part of this attitude of openness and discovery must also be an ecumenical aspect - the genus of this plant (*Buddleia*) is named after an Anglican clergyman, the Rev. Adam Buddle. Contemporary evangelisation cannot be about proselytism or 'sheep-stealing' but a co-operative, dialoguing movement of faith working with other Christians and all men and women of good will. In particular there is a need to recognise other Christians as partners not rivals as we work together to participate in the mission of God.[9] 'Mission and Unity' are not convenient administrative categories but the Good News includes and demands the unity of all Christ's faithful.

---

[8] See George Bishop, *Travels in Imperial China* (Cassell, London, 1996) for a popular account of aspects of the life of Père David.

[9] Cf. Pope John Paul II, *Redemptoris Missio* (1991) 1: 'The Council emphasized the Church's "missionary nature", basing it in a dynamic way on the Trinitarian mission itself. The missionary thrust therefore belongs to the very nature of the Christian life, and is also the inspiration behind ecumenism: "that they may all be one ... so that the world may believe that you have sent me"' (John 17:21).

The second stream in thinking around *Buddleia davidii* was to notice that it is both cultivated and also vital enough to seed itself without human intention. Many of us like to have the shrub in our gardens and enjoy it and the butterflies it attracts, yet this plant is so full of life, so willing to thrive that to keep it tidy for a suburban garden it needs regular and severe pruning. That vitality is such that it has gone wild, it appears all over the place. So too the Gospel cannot be contained: it will always find a place to belong. Yes, we must nurture the Gospel but we should also rejoice to spread the Good News. We must make our homes, and our ecclesial home, places where the Gospel flowers, but also we should celebrate when we see that of the Gospel making its own home even beyond our boundaries. One aspect of this is that in our present circumstances we are somewhere between 'Christendom' and 'Paganism'.[10] Our work is neither simply maintaining Christian structures within an entirely Christian society (marked perhaps by baptising infants on the presumption of their nurture in Christian homes within a Christian culture) nor are we within a ghetto where everything outside the visible bounds of the Church is anti-Christian. Our complex modern, post-modern, post-secular world is not so polarised but is partly Christian, partly Pagan yet all within the love of God. We may find grace blossoming in unexpected places.[11]

The third strand of thoughts kicked off by this plant is that it grows in the most marginal places. Evangelisation must have an orientation towards the margins and the marginalised. The Church must look beyond its boundaries. This includes an orientation which assists those who are outside the visible Church to become part of explicit company who know themselves to be God's people. Indeed, it must include activities that proclaim and present the person and work of Christ to those who are beyond our ecclesial margins.[12] But as well as this,

[10] Cf. Bishops' Conference, *On the Threshold* (M. James, 2000), p. 11.

[11] Cf. Vatican II, *Gaudium et Spes* 22: 'Through his incarnation the Son of God has united himself with every person.'

[12] Cf. Archbishop William Temple: 'The Church is the only society which exists for those who are not its members'; and Dietrich

there is a special location of the Gospel with those who are marginalised from society. Walking with the poorest and most deprived of our society has an imperative in the mission of the Church. The Gospel we are privileged to receive, share and see enacted must be 'Good News for the Poor'.[13]

The ethos of evangelisation

What is clear from our research, and perhaps not unexpected, is that many respondents understood evangelisation as simply *those activities which enabled those who were not Christians to become Christians*. (Question 49 of the survey: the largest response (49%) was to associate 'evangelisation' with making new Christians.) This is in itself a more holistic view than that held by those who would see evangelism[14] as only verbally proclaiming the Good News. Our view, which we believe also to be the teaching of the Catholic Church, is to see evangelisation on a wider frame than this.[15] Yet it is important to note this expectation. Growth in

---

Bonhöffer: 'The Church is only the Church when it exists for others'. Both quoted by David J. Bosch, *Transforming Mission* (Orbis, Maryknoll, 1991), p. 375.

[13] See below in the section on *Contextualisation* in the socio-economic context, and Pope John Paul II, *Novo Millennio Ineunte* (2001) 49f.

[14] See discussion below on the distinctions frequently met between *evangelisation* and *evangelism*.

[15] Cf. *Evangelii Nuntiandi* 17-18: 'In the Church's evangelizing activity there are of course certain elements and aspects to be specially insisted on. Some of them are so important that there will be a tendency simply to identify them with evangelization. Thus it has been possible to define evangelization in terms of proclaiming Christ to those who do not know Him, of preaching, of catechesis, of conferring Baptism and the other sacraments. Any partial and fragmentary definition which attempts to render the reality of evangelization in all its richness, complexity and dynamism does so only at the risk of impoverishing it and even of distorting it. It is impossible to grasp the concept of evangelization unless one tries to keep in view all its essential elements. ... For the Church, evangelizing means bringing the Good News into all the strata of humanity, and through its influence transforming humanity from within and making it new: "Now I am

numbers of practising Christians through proclaiming the central teachings of the Church is not only the most prevalent expectation of evangelisation, but is an essential component of evangelisation. A few objected to the sorts of questions we asked, condemning the sorts of things we were interested in as having nothing to do with evangelisation as seen from this perspective. We disagree with that but do affirm that evangelisation must proclaim the Good News of Christ with the purpose of making new Christians.

The image that many people have of evangelisation is that of helping a person who has no Christian identity or commitment move into full Christian identity and commitment. However, while acknowledging and affirming that image we would also note the variety of situations in which people find themselves and therefore the variety of routes of evangelisation. In addition, whilst the formation of new Christians is an essential fruit of evangelisation, there are other fruits which include the renewal of the Church and the transformation of human society. Thus we may see all the following, and more, as connected to evangelisation:

- The move from no Christian identity or commitment to full commitment. (The *unchurched*)
- The move from fringe Christian identity to full Christian identity. (The *partly churched*)
- The move from less active to more active faith and practice. (The renewal of faith of the *churched*)
- The gaining back of those who have chosen to leave the Church community, have rejected or been rejected by the Church, or have drifted away. (The *de-churched*)
- The deepening and renewal of existing active faith and practice, particularly in terms of ministries.
- The nurture and development of Christian children in Christian families situated in Christian communities.
- The nurture and development of Christian children in

---

making the whole of creation new". But there is no new humanity if there are not first of all new persons renewed by Baptism and by lives lived according to the Gospel.'

fringe or less active Christian families and situated in less clear Christian communities.

- The development of Christian communities as places of celebration, prayer, service and witness.
- The promotion of the fruits of the Gospel, such as love, justice and peace, amongst our neighbourhoods and society.

We were also very aware that there were a series of connected presuppositions which had collected as baggage around the term 'evangelisation' many of which seem based upon expectations of a previous generation of Evangelical evangelism rather than contemporary Catholic usage. Some thought 'evangelisation' a non-Catholic term, failing to recognise that it is one of the key and pressing teachings of the Catholic Church since Vatican II and of special concern to the present Pontiff. Yet these are not so much misconceptions, as not placing the emphasis of evangelisation where many Catholic workers in the field, in the UK and internationally, would do.

Consider the following table:

Presumptions often held about evangelisation	Mind of many workers in the field today
Convincing people about doctrinal arguments	• Entering into relationships
Big events (e.g. Billy Graham crusades)	• Value of small groups and local communities
Conversion event	• Development process and journey
Intellectual decision of individual	• Holistic growth with others
Dramatic and sudden	• Gentle and gradual
Evangelists as teachers	• Evangelists as witnesses
Work of professionals	• Work of all Christians
Imposing 'truth'	• Sharing spirituality in dialogue
Answering Protestant objections to Catholicism: converting non-Catholics	• Working together with other Christians in common commitment to mission and unity
Lecture	• Celebration
Other worldly focus	• Integrated with daily life, including the search for Justice and Peace
Telling people about Christianity	• Experiencing living Christianity

The left-hand column seems to be consistent with the experience and perceptions of many of our survey respondents: the right-hand column attempts to synthesise the feelings of many of those whom we talked to as 'participant observers' of evangelisation agencies and initiatives. These two columns are not mutually exclusive and certainly we are not suggesting that the Church should abandon 'right teaching'. However, there may be trends here worth thinking through. The issue is one of methods more than doctrines. Growth in understanding the propositions that the Church holds as true happens through experiencing the life of faith, which those propositions seek to express.

That being said, we must report that many of our respondents expressed a desire for the promotion of clear teaching on doctrinal and moral issues. Amongst issues identified were the Real Presence of Christ in the Eucharist, reticence on pro-life issues and sexual morality. We acknowledge and wish to take seriously this concern that the core dogmas of the Church seem to have been downplayed. Several respondents articulated worries about the content of teaching in Catholic schools. Several praised the *Catechism of the Catholic Church* and wished for it to have a more central place in the presentation of Catholic faith and practice. However, we must also report that other respondents expressed a concern that the Catholic Church was too dogmatic and rule-bound. Concern was expressed for the pastoral care of gay men and women and divorced and remarried Catholics. Others have told of the deep rejection felt by some non-Catholic partners married to Catholics.

The ethos of evangelisation as a crusade based on the primary presentation of doctrinal teaching which individuals needed to accept is very different from where most evangelisation is today. The ethos of evangelisation in England and Wales in our time must be about shared experiences and lives of faith in welcoming local communities, it must be human and humane, personal and relational. The personal relationship of the believer with God in Christ must be a fundamental focus.

It does seem appropriate to distinguish evangelisation from evangelism even if many would treat them as direct synonyms. Evangelism and evangelisation can be unified as being concerned with the spread of the Gospel. An important ecumenical dialogue could note: '"Evangelism" and "evangelization" are used indiscriminately in this Report. The former is more common among Evangelicals, the latter among Roman Catholics, but both words describe the same activity of spreading the gospel.'[16]

Yet the same report would continue to examine many tensions within that 'same activity of spreading the gospel' over which Evangelicals and Catholics may be distinguished. Beyond the eirenic sphere of ecumenical dialogue, the similarity of language hides significant disagreement. Some will limit evangelism to the verbal proclamation of the Gospel, others will extend evangelisation to include all activity connected with the Gospel including personal conversion, ecclesial renewal and social transformation.

Evangelism is most commonly a noun of action associated in English usage with the Churches of the Reformation: Catholics have preferred the parallel lexical structure of *Evangelisation*. In terms of word structure the former reflects historical Greek uses of creating a noun from a verb and the latter a Latin source. Whatever the etymology, present uses suggest both an overlap of a field of meaning yet also some distinction between these. Both nouns necessarily imply activity which is *en-gospelling*[17]. Such nouns must gain their import from the actions represented. Some would narrowly proscribe these actions, others incorporate a wider scope of activity. As a rule of thumb evangelisation tends to refer to a wider and more comprehensive set of actions than evangelism.[18] Both

[16] Basil Meeking and John Stott (ed), *The Evangelical/Roman Catholic Dialogue on Mission 1977-1984* (The Paternoster Press, Exeter, 1986), note 1, p. 95.

[17] English usage finds such verbal nouns awkward, but clumsy forms such as *en-gospelling* or *Good-Newsing* may best express the weight of evangelisation.

[18] However, some from the Churches of the Reformation will use 'evangelism' with a wider remit. See the debate between two representatives of different strands of Methodism in Brian Hoare and Leslie Griffiths, 'A Decade of Evangelism - or Evangelisation', *Epworth Review* 19 (1), January 1992, pp. 68-79.

evangelism and evangelisation include the action of the announcement or proclamation of the Good News and the linked notion of giving witness. In most uses this proclamation is extended to the active persuasion and conviction of those who are not Christians to become Christians. Evangelisation may also include the state of having had the Gospel proclaimed and indeed the state of the Gospel being accepted and transforming individuals and societies.[19] However, the notion of conversion or transformation also allows for an understanding of a process, in addition to or in place of a single event. Thus the continuing growth of the Christian in faith may be considered as part of evangelisation, as is the deepening and revivification of Christian communities. Therefore, catechesis, spiritual direction and ecclesial and parish renewal may also be components of (and/or factors in) evangelisation. We shall argue that it is also a further legitimate and proper extension of the verbal noun evangelisation to include within its semantic depth the enactment of Good News. That is to say that proclamation and persuasion become meaningful through the establishment of the things that they announce and of which they convince their hearers. Not only are we to talk of the liberation of the captives but we must liberate them: the message is not simply to be spoken but realised. In this sense there must be an actualisation of Good News for the proclamation and persuasion to be authentic. Thus *Evangelii Nuntiandi* declared:

> For the Church, evangelisation means bringing the Good News into all strata of humanity, and through its influence transforming humanity from within and making it new.[20]

[19] In some Evangelical usage evangelisation may be distinguished from evangelism on this basis: evangelism is the activity or activities of proclaiming the Gospel, evangelisation is the result of the proclamation and its acceptance.

[20] *Evangelii Nuntiandi* 18.

The biblical background to evangelisation

Evangelisation is not itself a biblical term, yet has an intimate connection with key scriptural concepts and is consciously derived from key New Testament Greek words. In various ways the scriptural concepts of *Gospel*, *Proclaiming the Gospel* and *Proclaimer of the Gospel* feed into the understanding of evangelisation. The literary genre of Gospel and the derived concept of evangelist as writer of such a literary genre underline the necessary concept of communication within the understanding of evangelisation. The writing of the Gospels was in itself part of the process of evangelisation by the sub-apostolic Church. These writings communicate to the world the message and messenger of the Gospel: 'the Good News of Jesus Christ, the Son of God' (Mark 1:1). It is worth emphasising here that the debate over whether the genitive *Iesou Christou* is subjective or objective allows for both the *Jerusalem Bible* translation 'the Good News about Jesus Christ' (Christ as message) and the *Revised Standard Version* 'Good News of Jesus Christ' (Christ as messenger),

    There is a secular Greek use of *evangelion* and *evangelos* most usually as news of military victory and the bringer of news of victory or indeed *evangelion* as the reward received by the messenger. *Evangelos* also has a religious meaning as the one who delivers an oracle. We may also note a connection with the imperial cult; *evangelion* applies to the birth of the emperor as a divine man and at other key moments in his life. The new intervention of the divine in the affairs of humanity by the coming of the imperial God-Man is declared to be Good News.[21] In all these the Good News is a statement of what is more than a hope for what will be: it is what has been done, not an invitation to do something.

    Bsr as a Hebrew root contains within itself the general sense of proclaiming good news (e.g. 1 Kings 1:42, the coronation of

---

[21] See Gerhard Friedrich in Gerhard Kittel, *Theological Dictionary of the New Testament* (Wm Eeerdmans, Grand Rapids, Michigan, 1964) vol. II, p. 723f.

Solomon; 2 Kings 7:9, the lifting of the siege of Samaria); the concept of joy is within the stem itself. This frequently has the character of announcing what is, even to the point of creating that which is announced by the act of announcement. Perhaps the most fertile source for New Testament usage comes from Duetero-Isaiah and the notion of herald, the bringer of good news, *M'basser*.

> He is the herald who precedes the people on its return from Babylon to Sion. ...
>
> He proclaims the victory of Yahweh over the whole world. Yahweh is now returning to Sion to rule. The messenger publishes it, and the new age begins.
>
> He does not declare that the rule of God will soon commence; he proclaims it, he publishes it, and it comes into effect. Salvation comes with the word of proclamation. By the fact that he declares the restoration of Israel, the new creation of the world, the inauguration of the eschatalogical age, he brings them to pass. For the word is not just breath and sound; it is effective power.[22]

The bearer of Good News is also the creator of Good News. This double-edged nature of the proclamation of Good News will be a major argument for us. The public proclamation of what is, enacts what is proclaimed. The herald carries the word of the Lord on his lips. It is God who speaks and that speech brings into effect that of which it speaks:

> Yes, as the rain and the snow come down from the heavens and do not return without watering the earth, making it yield and giving growth to provide seed for the sower and bread for the eating so the word that goes from my mouth does not return to me empty, without carrying out my will and succeeding in what it was sent to do.
>
> Isaiah 55:10-11

[22] Friedrich, p. 708.

The messenger of good news in Deutero-Isaiah has a close connection with the New Testament concepts of Gospel and proclamation of the Gospel. Both have eschatalogical expectations, both announce that God is actively ruling, both broaden salvation history to include the Gentiles, both offer a critique of contemporary religious practice and both give weight to ideas of righteousness, salvation and peace. Hellenistic Judaism may have weakened this link: the proclamation of the message was separated from the action contained within it. However, Rabbinic Judaism maintained and extended the notion of bringer of Good News, either as the Messiah or a forerunner to the Messiah, and his proclamation of the message.[23]

In the New Testament the notion of *evangelion* is made central through the writing of Paul. It is unlikely to be part of the language of the historical Jesus but belongs to apostolic Christian reflection.[24] Most of the 76 occurrences of *evangelion* in the New Testament are in the writings of Paul. Luke's Gospel does not use the noun at all (although Acts uses it twice). The verb *evangelizo* appears largely in Luke/Acts and Paul. Neither noun nor verb occurs in the fourth Gospel.

Jesus is the one who both brings the good news of the expected last time and brings about the expected last time. Evangelisation is therefore necessarily about the person of Jesus and the acts of Jesus as well as the teaching of Jesus. In answer to the disciples of John the Baptist and their question of whether he was the 'one who is to come', Jesus says:

> Go back and tell John what you hear and see; the blind see again, and the lame walk, lepers are cleansed, and the deaf hear, and the dead are raised to life and the Good News is proclaimed to the poor.
>
> Matthew 11:5 (Luke 7:22)

---

[23] See U. Becker in Colin Brown, *New International Dictionary of New Testament Theology* (Paternoster Press, Exeter, 1976) vol. II, p. 109.

[24] See Friedrich, p. 727f.

The climax of the message is the Good News being preached to the poor. This confirms Jesus as Christ in images familiar from Deutero-Isaiah and Rabbinic Judaism. 'The message actualises the new time and makes possible the signs of Messianic fulfilment. The Word brings in the divine rule.'[25] Proclamation is both word and deed. This is clearly seen in the opening accounts of the ministry of Jesus in both Mark and Luke. Mark begins with the simple statement:

> After John had been arrested, Jesus went into Galilee. There he proclaimed the Good News from God. 'The time has come,' he said, 'and the kingdom of God is close at hand. Repent, and believe the Good News.'
>
> Mark 1:14-15

The Good News is that in Jesus the time has come for the ruling of God to be made manifest. Jesus brings in the kingdom of God. From his coming the kingdom is inaugurated. It is made actual in him. Jesus not only heralds this kingdom, it is established in him and his actions. This Gospel is salvation for all creation and must be offered to all people (Mark 16:15).Yet this message and messenger still demands a response. While at one level the proclamation is saying what is, what God has done and is doing, there remains a demand for faith from the hearers of the word. The Good News is offered to those who repent and believe. People must receive the Good News, and turn around to live the new life of the kingdom. It is to be actualised in transformed lives.

Luke establishes the nature of the ministry of Christ by quotation from Trito-Isaiah:

> Unrolling the scroll Jesus found the place where it is written:
> *The spirit of the Lord has been given to me, for he has anointed me.*
> *He has sent me to bring the good news to the poor, to proclaim liberty*
> *to captives and to the blind new sight, to set the downtrodden free, to*
> *proclaim the Lord's year of favour.*

[25] Friedrich, p. 718.

He then rolled up the scroll, gave it back to the assistant and sat down. And all eyes in the synagogue were fixed on him. then he began to speak to them, 'This text is being fulfilled today even as you listen'.

Luke 4:17-20

This places the ministry of Jesus as a fulfilment of the Old Testament. There is an eschatological realisation in announcing that this prophetic discourse is being fulfilled. The last days have arrived in Jesus; this is the time of salvation, 'the Lord's year of favour'. Works and words proclaim and enact Good News. This Good News brings not simply personal conversion but also social transformation. The Jubilee promise brings healing and forgiveness both to sinners and the victims of sin and structures of sin. The news of restoration restores. Evangelising establishes the Gospel in human lives. Diseases are cured (e.g. Matthew 4:23, 9:35), the excluded are welcomed back (e.g. Matthew 11:5), human relationships with God are made right (e.g. Acts 10:36).

The Good News that Jesus brings and brings about has been given to the followers of Jesus to share with others. The 'great commission' (Matthew 28:16-20) sets the work of the Church in an eschatological context. Because all authority in heaven and earth has been given to Christ, **therefore** the eleven are sent out to all nations to make disciples, and this happens with the assurance that Jesus is with them always, until the end of time. The work of Jesus continues with the work of the Church. The Gospel the Church is to preach is Jesus. Their task is to take his Good News - to take him - into all the world. The interim period between the inauguration and consummation of the kingdom is characterised by the mission of the Church. The Church's mission 'fills the present and keeps the walls of history apart.'[26]

[26] Bosch's translation of Hoekendijk in Bosch, p. 503. Even if we draw back from the radical eschatology of the 'Salvation History' school associated with the early writings of Oscar Cullman, evangelisation must have an eschatalogical component. See below the discussion on *missio Dei*.

To preach the Gospel is not simply to speak to others. In its proclamation is power; it brings into effect the age of grace, the rule of God. Healing and forgiveness accompany the manifestation of God's Good News in Jesus. The apostles in Acts 14 demonstrate this. Paul and Barnabas in Iconium preached boldly for the Lord, 'and the Lord supported all that they said about his gift of grace, allowing signs and wonders to be performed by them' (Acts 14:3). The healing of a crippled man (in Lystra?) is integral to the preaching of the Good News (Acts 14:8-18). One important consequence, but not the only one, is that at Derbe they 'made a considerable number of disciples' (Acts 14:21). Social justice (indeed a redistribution greater than simple justice) characterises the community founded by the Gospel (Acts 2:42-47, 4:32-35, cf. Galatians 2:10)

The Gospel is Jesus and what God in Jesus has done, which is present in the world and presented to people in the world so that the world, in all its dimensions, may be saved. This is developed most fully by Paul. The Gospel is preached by Paul to both those who have no relationship with Christ and to those who are followers of Christ (Romans 1:8-15). The preaching of the Gospel is God speaking to all people and revealing himself to all in grace and judgement. The heart of the Gospel is Jesus, his incarnation, life, suffering, death and resurrection. The Gospel is the manifestation of the glory of God in history through Jesus (cf. 2 Corinthians 4:4). The lens through which all this is interpreted is the crucifixion (1 Corinthians 1:17). The cross is the climax of salvation history, the open secret of God, now being revealed by the power of God (1 Corinthians 2:19). This mystery gives the faithful strength to live according to the Gospel (Romans 16:25-27).

The Gospel establishes communities and bears fruits (1 Corinthians 15:1, Colossians 1:5). Those who are obedient to the Gospel are active in service and love. The evangelised community experiences in its life the gift and grace of God (2 Corinthians 9:13-15). The Gospel is a life-giving force which transforms history, people and communities.

The Gospel does not merely bear witness to salvation history; it is itself salvation history. It breaks into the life of man, refashions it and creates communities. The Gospel is not an empty word; it is effective power which brings to pass what it says because God is its author.[27]

It is this effective word which must characterise evangelisation. It is indeed the verbal and non-verbal proclamation of the Good News but evangelisation is also the actualisation of the things being proclaimed. In this those who serve the Gospel are empowered to be instruments of the Gospel. In the announcement of the Gospel, that which is announced is realised.

Evangelisation in recent Catholic usage

'Evangelisation' was not introduced as a neologism in the 1970s but it did appear, almost without explanation, as the preferred term in post-conciliar discussions.[28] A cursory glance at the *Catholic Periodical and Literature Index* shows an absence of the term in 1967-1968, its appearance in 1969-1970 and its frequent use by the 1973-1974 edition. This may well be because it was a more natural term to use in non-English speaking Europe. Indeed the verb *evangelizare* is used in the Vulgate. However, it may also be that as a term it escaped the baggage of the alternatives. Both *mission* and *evangelism*[29] carried with them fields of meaning and associations, which the post-conciliar debate wished to move beyond.

[27] Friedrich, p. 731.
[28] See Karl Miffier SVD, 'Missiology an introduction' in Sebastian Karotemprel, *Following Christ in Mission: A Foundational Course in Missiology* (Paulines Publications, Africa, Nairobi, 1995), p. 29.
[29] *Evangelismo* did exist in Italian and *evangelisme* in French to describe a movement of religious reform calling for greater adherence to the life of Christ in the Spirit of the Gospel associated with Imbart de la Tour. See *Dictionario Ecclesiastico* I, (Unione Tipografico, Torino, 1953), p. 1041. However, this use was not widespread.

Mission was seen to be associated with colonialism and to be concerned with the administration of missions distinct from the normative hierarchical pattern.[30] There was a severe crisis of confidence about the nature of mission at the close of the colonial era. Missions had been part of the matrix of imperialism; Eurocentric patterns had been imposed upon 'natives' which often seemed to have more to do with the promulgation of European culture than the spread of the Gospel. The post-conciliar era of emphasising dialogue, development, liberation and inculturation shifted the nature of missionary activity in the non-European world. At the same time the acknowledgement of secularisation and secularism and the decline in religious adherence in areas where the Church had been long established demanded a new focus on missionary activity in Europe and elsewhere. There was a growing sense of crisis in mission *ad gentes* and concern about falling vocations and decline in religious practice. A new concept, or at least a revived concept with new implications, would help stress the demands on the Church at this time. In addition evangelisation has greater scriptural resonance than that of mission.

Evangelism was commonly used in English speaking non-Catholic circles and had a particular reference to verbal proclamation, evangelistic rallies and individual conviction of sin and acceptance of the Gospel. In addition to this the 'universal sinfulness and guilt of fallen man'[31] and the general perspective of a sharp distinction between the worldly sphere and the world of grace associated with Evangelical evangelism were alien to the Catholic tradition. Indeed since Vatican II a positive approach to anthropology, human cultures and religions has built on existing Catholic natural theology and understandings of the action of grace. There is also a greater sense of the cosmic and the corporate in Catholic evangelisation than is to be found in the frequent individual emphasis in non-Catholic evangelism.

---

[30] See the discussion in the chapter on *missio Dei* below.
[31] Basis of Faith of Evangelical Alliance:
{www.eauk.org/beliefs/basisoffaith.htm}.

It is worth returning to the 1977-1984 Report on Evangelical/Roman Catholic dialogue on mission. Although this document does use evangelism and evangelisation interchangeably, it is clear that the Catholic participants tend to understand a wider remit:

> Vatican II defines the Church for Roman Catholics as 'the sacrament of salvation', the sign and promise of redemption to each and every person without exception. For them therefore, 'mission' includes not only evangelization but also the service of human need, and the building up and expression of fellowship in the Church.[32] It is the mission of the Church to anticipate the Kingdom of God as liberation from the slavery of sin, from slavery to the Law and from death; by the preaching of the gospel, by the forgiveness of sins and by sharing in the Lord's Supper. But the Spirit of God is always at work throughout human history to bring about the liberating reign of God.
>
> Evangelization is the proclamation (by word and example) of the good news to the nations. The good news is that God's actions in Jesus Christ are the climax of a divine revelation and relationship that has been made available to everyone from the beginning. Roman Catholics assert that the whole of humanity is a collective history which God makes to be a history of salvation. The *mysterion* of the gospel is the announcement by the Church to the world of this merging of the history of salvation with the history of the world.
>
> Evangelicals generally, on the other hand, do not regard the history of salvation as coterminous with the history of the world, although some are struggling with this question. The Church is the beginning and anticipation of the new creation, the firstborn among his creatures. Though all in Adam die, not all are automatically in Christ. So life in Christ has to be received by grace with repentance through faith. With yearning

---

[32] Although this statement presumes evangelisation to be part of a wider phenomenon, mission, it must be noted that such a distinction is often blurred.

Evangelicals plead for a response to the atoning work of Christ
in his death and resurrection. But with sorrow they know not all
who are called are chosen. Judgment (both here and hereafter)
is the divine reaction of God to sin and the rejection of the good
news. 'Rich young rulers' still walk away from the kingdom of
grace. Evangelization is therefore the call to those outside to
come as children of the Father into the fullness of eternal life in
Christ by the Spirit and into the joy of a loving community in
the fellowship of the Church.[33]

The Catholic participants here intimately connected the
service of human need and the building up of fellowship in the
Church with evangelisation. In this they follow a frequent
missiological pattern of connecting the mission of the Church
with three New Testament Greek words: *kerygma* - apostolic
preaching; *diakonia* - service of Church and neighbour; *koinonia* -
communion, participation and fellowship both with God
(including sacramental communion) and with other people.
Variations of these have floated around in ecumenical
missionary circles for most of the past fifty years and have been
taken up by many Catholic missiologists.[34] In addition there is
an anticipatory aspect to the Catholic understanding
underpinned by sacramental theology. However, the most sharp
distinction is over the nature of history and salvation history:
Catholics affirm the collective nature of human history and the
merging of the history of salvation with that history. There is a
universality to the Catholic conception of evangelisation in
which all that is human is touched by the Good News.

In the years after the council there developed a wide
understanding of evangelisation. Whereas before (and often
after) the council many would specify 'evangelisation' as

---

[33] *The Evangelical/Roman Catholic Dialogue on Mission 1977-1984*, p.
30f.

[34] See Bosch, p. 511f. Adrian Hastings, 'The diversities of Mission',
Missionalia 24 (1) 1996, pp. 3-16. See also Madge Karechi, 'A Missing
Link: A Response to Adrian Hastings' irreducible triangle of the
Church', *Missionalia* 25 (1) 1997, pp. 124-134.

referring only to missionary preaching[35] - at times during and after the council it included nearly everything the Church did. The second draft of the *Instrumentum Laboris* for the 1974 Synod of bishops offered this definition:

> By 'evangelization' therefore is meant every activity ... whereby the People of God arouses and fosters a living faith. In this activity three tasks of the Church have to be considered in particular, *viz.* preaching of the Word, testimony of life and administration of the sacraments because they excel among various aspects of evangelization.[36]

Word, deed and liturgy combine in evangelisation: *kerygma*, *diakonia* and *koinonia* co-operate in the one task of arousing and fostering a living faith. Although this has a wide vision, there is a focus upon transmission of faith within which many of the Church's activities are involved. Indeed one could argue that all the Church's activities impinge directly or indirectly on this. Although some activities may seem to have priorities other than the transmission of faith, nonetheless Canon Law, pastoral care, prayer and liturgy, care of the sick, social teaching and activism and other activities all contribute to this comprehensive activity of evangelisation. If the mission of the Church is all that the Father, through the Son and in the Holy Spirit has sent the Church to do, then all of this activity touches to some degree on the task of spreading the Good News. The character of evangelisation is arousing and fostering faith in the Gospel and enabling the Gospel to be actualised: the scope of this touches all that is human.

This synod discussed many aspects of evangelisation. These included: the need for the self-evangelisation of the Church

---

[35] For instance, 'By the term "evangelization" we mean the proclamation of the Gospel to non-Christians with the aim of faith and conversion, and with the consequent incorporation into the Church through baptism'. D. Grassi in SEDOS, *Foundations of Mission Theology* (Orbis, Maryknoll NY, 1972), p. 108.

[36] Quoted by Jan L. Witte SJ in Mariasusai Dhavamony, *Evangelisation* (Documenta Missionalia 9, Università Gregoriana, Rome, 1975), p. 222f.

herself;[37] the need for evangelisation to be 'of the whole man as it is for all men';[38] the continuing importance of 'the oral and verbal Proclamation of the explicit announcement of Jesus Christ';[39] the imperative that 'the announcement of good news ought to be an interpretation of the concrete human existence of people according to the Gospel'.[40] Thus:

> To evangelize then is to come back to the newness and originality of the Gospel, to recapture the specificity of the Gospel message as a witness and a call to the universal love demonstrated by God to men in Jesus Christ. The work of evangelization demands therefore of the Church that she be faithful in listening to and meditating upon the Word of God, that she be given to prayer and contemplation, that she lives a true life of the Spirit.[41]

The outworking of this demands dialogue with others, to seek for seeds of God's words amongst those encountered beyond the Church. This includes those who in their lives give a witness to elements of the Gospel. Amongst such elements must be social transformation. The 1974 synod quoted a previous (1971) Synod of Bishops:

> [A]ction on behalf of Justice, and participation in the transformation of the world fully appears to us as a constitutive dimension of the preaching of the Gospel - or in other words, of the Church's mission for the redemption of the human race and its liberation from every oppressive situation.[42]

---

[37] Synthesis of Part I: Sharing of experiences prepared by Rev. D. S. Amalorpavadass and presented by Cardinal J. Cordeiro, 4 October 1974, based on 5 Continental relations and 108 interventions, in D. S. Amalorpavadass, *Evangelisation in the Modern World* (National Biblical Catechetical and Litrugical Centre, Bangalore), p. 95.

[38] Amalorpavadass, p. 98f.

[39] Amalorpavadass, p. 99.

[40] Amalorpavadass, p. 99.

[41] Amalorpavadass, p. 99.

[42] Amalorpavadass, p. 102.

This was presented in the context of integral human development and the particular demands of poverty and underdevelopment. It affirmed the need for social transformation while also affirming that there were other dimensions to humanity.

The Apostolic Exhortation *Evangelii Nuntiandi* sought a synthesis of several issues raised by the synod. At the request of the synod, Paul VI built on their discussions in order to stimulate 'a new and more fruitful era of evangelization'.[43] Most germane to our purposes, the Apostolic Exhortation sought to answer the question, 'What is Evangelization?'[44]

The work of evangelisation is a continuation in the Church of the mission of Christ and an ongoing encounter with Christ through the Church. Indeed the origin and nature of the Church is in the mission of Christ and its continuation.[45] Christ announced the kingdom of God[46] and proclaimed salvation[47] and that these could be achieved in every person, particularly by the radical conversion of the whole person (*metanoia*).[48] Those who are evangelised by this Good News, which is the message of Jesus, his person and actions, themselves become evangelisers.[49] This important dual point must be stressed: the Church exists because of evangelisation and the Church exists in order to evangelise. The Divine Son evangelised and evangelises. The Holy Spirit evangelised and evangelises. It is through the encounter with the Good News incarnated by the Son and inspired by the Spirit that people and the people of God are evangelised. The Church takes part in this. Evangelisation by the people of God is a necessary consequence of their own personal and corporate evangelisation:

[43] *Evangelii Nuntiandi* 2.
[44] *Evangelii Nuntiandi* ch. 2, 17-24, see also ch. 3, 'The Message of Evangelization', 25-39.
[45] *Evangelii Nuntiandi* 14-15.
[46] *Evangelii Nuntiandi* 7.
[47] *Evangelii Nuntiandi* 8.
[48] *Evangelii Nuntiandi* 9.
[49] Cf. *Evangelii Nuntiandi* 15, 24.

The Church's fundamental task is simultaneously to be evangelized and to evangelize, both to become and to share the good news.[50]

Evangelisation is not simply something that the Church does, but something which happens to the Church. The Good News of God in Christ, the kingdom of God, salvation and all the other key concepts are things which the Church must receive as well as transmit.

Those who accept the Good News of Jesus with all its transforming power, are transformed into those who become mediators and transmitters of that Good News.

> Those who sincerely accept the good news, by virtue of it and the faith which it generates, are united in the name of Jesus so that they may together seek the kingdom, build it up and implement it in their own lives. In this way they establish community which becomes itself a herald of the gospel. ... 'The church exists to preach the gospel' - that is to preach and teach the word of God so that through her the gift of grace may be given to us, sinners may be reconciled to God, and the sacrifice of the Mass, the memorial of his glorious death and resurrection, may be perpetuated.[51]

This echoes the conciliar understanding that the very nature of the Church is missionary, being formed by and in the mission of the triune God who both reaches out to all people and draws all people to himself.[52]

The nature of evangelisation is presented as a comprehensive, if complex, whole. The temptation to identify any single activity connected with evangelisation as the whole of evangelisation, is firmly resisted, but a broad and inclusive

[50] Mgr. David Bohr, 'Becoming and Sharing the Good News: the Nature and Content of Evangelization' in Kenneth Boyack CSP (ed.), *Catholic Evangelization Today: A New Pentecost for the United States* (Paulist Press, New York/Mahwah, 1987), p. 42.

[51] *Evangelii Nuntiandi* 13-14.

[52] Vatican II, *Ad Gentes* 2.

panorama of the depths of the human condition is addressed. The following extract may represent the fullest definition of evangelisation:

> In the Church's work of evangelization there are undoubtedly certain elements and aspects which are deserving of special attention. Some of these are indeed of such importance that they may at times be regarded as constituting in themselves the whole of evangelization. Thus, for example, evangelization has been defined as consisting in the proclamation of Christ Our Lord to those who do not know him, in preaching, catechetics, baptism and the administration of the other sacraments. But no such defective and incomplete definition can be accepted for that complex, rich and dynamic reality which is called evangelization without the risk of weakening or even distorting its real meaning. ....
>
> The Church appreciates that evangelization means the carrying forth of the good news to every sector of the human race so that by its strength it may enter into the hearts of men and renew the human race. ... In a word the Church may be truly said to evangelize when, solely in virtue of the news which she proclaims, she seeks to convert both the individual consciences of men and their collective conscience, all the activities in which they are engaged and, finally, their lives and the whole environment which surrounds them. ... Evangelization is to be achieved, not from without as though by adding some decoration or applying a coat of colour, but in depth, going to the very centre and roots of life. The gospel must impregnate the culture and the whole way of life of man, taking these words in the widest and fullest sense which they are given in the constitution *Gaudium et Spes.* This work must always take the human person as its starting point, coming back to the interrelationships between persons and their relation with God.[53]

---

[53] *Evangelii Nuntiandi*, 17-18, 20.

Several strands cohere in an integrated whole here. Word and deed transmit the Good News. 'The Word must not only be proclaimed; it must also be celebrated and lived.'[54] Both the person and society are the location for evangelisation.[55] All that is human, individual consciences, activities, lives, cultures and the whole environment is converted, renewed and transformed by the Gospel.

The goal and result of evangelisation is the 'new creation'[56], the new humanity which the Holy Spirit establishes through universal grace. Essential elements in the life of the Church which support this process include:

- a renewal of human nature,
- witness,
- public proclamation,
- wholehearted acceptance of the Church,
- entrance into the community of the Church,
- acceptance of outward signs of faith,
- apostolic works.[57]

The missionary mandate of Jesus to evangelize has various aspects, all of which, however, are closely connected with each other: 'proclaim' (Mark 16:15), 'make disciples and teach' (cf. Matthew 28:19-20), 'baptize' (Acts 1:8), 'do this in memory of me' (Luke 22:19), 'love one another' (John 15:12). Proclamation, witness, teaching, sacraments, love of neighbour: all of these aspects are the means by which the one Gospel is transmitted and they constitute the essential elements of evangelization itself. ... Evangelization ... must develop its 'totality' and

[54] Shorter, p. 7. He expands this in a series of triads. 'Evangelization comprises proclamation, praxis and prayer' (p. 8) or 'word, witness and worship' (p. 20).

[55] Cf. 'To evangelize means making Christ present in the life of man as a person and at the same time in the life of society', Pope John Paul II, General Audience, 21 February 1979, in *Reflections on Puebla* (CIIR, London, 1980), p. 44.

[56] *Evangelii Nuntiandi* 75.

[57] *Evangelii Nuntiandi* 24.

completely incorporate its intrinsic bipolarity: witness and proclamation, word and sacrament, interior change and social transformation.[58]

Such a wide scope for evangelisation was taken up by many as a positive development.[59] For many Societies of Apostolic Life and others this enabled a renewal of their charism and apostolate by focussing their activities on human experiences, cultures and needs.[60] The proper duty to be in solidarity with the poor and work for social transformation has become central to the work of many throughout the world. Respectful dialogue with men and women of good will, in the political and social

[58] Congregation for the Clergy, *General Directory for Catechesis* (1997) 46.

[59] Consider Bernard Häring, *Evangelization Today* (St Paul Publications, Slough, 1990), p. 1. 'The term "evangelization" is understood in the larger sense of testimony and proclamation of the mystery of salvation, not only as propagation of the faith, but also as its perennial deepening and vitalization.'

[60] See Mary Motte FMM, 'The Poor: Starting Point for Mission' in Geraid H. Anderson, James M. Phillips and Robert T. Coote (ed.), *Mission in the 1990s* (Eerdmans, Grand Rapids, 1991), p. 50-52. Cf. the Mission Statement of the Mill Hill Missionaries: 'We are an international fellowship of priests, lay members and associates. Since our foundation in 1866 by Cardinal Vaughan of Westminster, London, we have been serving the poor and destitute of the world, both spiritually and materially. Today some 650 of us are still active in this service of love. We have heard the words of Christ to his disciples: "Go therefore, make disciples of all nations, baptise them in the name of the Father and of the Son and of the Holy Spirit, and teach them to observe all the commands I gave you". Together, as a Society, we are committed to acting on these words. We believe that the Kingdom of God is the pearl of great value and that the Gospel is the power of God saving all who have faith. To receive this gift ourselves, we set out hearts on God's Kingdom and righteousness. To share this gift with others, we have freely left our homes, our relatives and friends and become, like the apostles, witnesses to Christ proclaiming the Good News to peoples "far away". True to our missionary vocation, we are ready to leave our country and our own culture. We do so in order that the Gospel of Christ may bring together people of different races and may become incarnate in every culture and nation.' {www.millhillmissionaries.org}

sphere, in the arts and sciences, amongst other religious traditions, with psychologists, therapists and elsewhere, has stimulated many Christians and has indeed been an encounter in the world with the Gospel. Love of neighbour has led to many fruitful initiatives. However, such an entirely legitimate broadening of the scope and perception of the Church's mission may also have led to a downplay of the aspect of actively making new Christians.

> Nevertheless, also as a result of the changes which have taken place in modern times and the spread of new theological ideas, some people wonder: Is missionary work among non-Christians still relevant? Has it not been replaced by inter-religious dialogue? Is not human development an adequate goal of the Church's mission? Does not respect for conscience and for freedom exclude all efforts at conversion? Is it not possible to attain salvation in any religion? Why then should there be missionary activity?[61]

Whereas the immediate post-conciliar generation broadened the scope of evangelisation to more than forming new Christians, the danger identified here is that this broadening may involve a move away from forming new Christians. More recent documents of the Magisterium have tended to be more specific concerning the agenda of evangelisation. Without abandoning the wider perspective of *Evangelii Nuntiandi*, nonetheless the priority of the Church's 'missionary thrust towards non-Christians' has been affirmed.[62] There is no narrowing the conception of evangelisation to simply 'the proclamation of Christ Our Lord to those who do not know him, in preaching, catechetics, baptism and the administration of the other sacraments' (the definition which *Evangelii Nuntiandi* described as defective and incomplete) but the documents associated with John Paul II have re-affirmed the necessity of

[61] *Redemptoris Missio* 4
[62] *Redemptoris Missio* 2.

this aspect of evangelisation. Evangelisation must comprise more than just this, but this must be included.

The final recent strand building on the above which must contribute to our present understanding of evangelisation is the development of the concept of 'New Evangelisation'. This takes seriously the contexts in which evangelisation today takes place. The term has grown to describe the ongoing response of the Church working in areas (territorial, cultural and social) where the Gospel has already been proclaimed and to some degree accepted. However, the demands of the present force a renewal of evangelisation.

The phrase has been something of a *leitmotif* in the pontificate of John Paul II. In discussing the needs of the Latin American Church 500 years after the arrival of the first Christian missionaries to that continent he exhorted:

> Look to the future with commitment to a New Evangelization, one that is new in its ardour, new in its methods, and new in its means of expression.[63]

Similar calls were made earlier to the Churches of Africa[64] and Europe.[65] The notion is not that evangelisation itself is novel: there has been evangelisation of various sorts in all these and other places. Rather, contemporary needs demand new initiatives in evangelisation renewed in zeal, open to try new techniques and finding appropriate new ways of articulating the unchanging Good News. Imperial conquest of the Americas is not appropriate as a model of evangelisation today (and indeed has left many scars, which the Church must now seek to

---

[63] 'The Task of the Latin American Bishops', *Origins* 12 (24 March 1983), p. 661.

[64] E.g. Homily at Mass at Cotonou (Benin) reported in *L'Osservatore Romano (Weekly English Edition)*, 1 March 1982, p. 4. See also both the *ad limina* visit of the Nigerian Bishops to Rome in *L'Osservatore Romano (Weekly English Edition)*, 1 February 1982, p. 18f., and addresses in Nigeria, e.g. *L'Osservatore Romano (Weekly English Edition)*, 22 February 1982, p. 12.

[65] *L'Osservatore Romano (Weekly English Edition)*, 8 February 1982, p. 9.

heal[66]). Post-Enlightenment, Modern and post-Modern Europe provide a different context and potential for evangelisation than the world of Augustine of Canterbury or Boniface. Aware of the past, the present must take seriously its own concerns. The Church must engage with contemporary needs by responding to, living and presenting the Gospel in a way that touches contemporary women and men.

This confirms our initial observations that the contexts and circumstances of those who hear the Word influence the manner in which the Word is proclaimed. To talk of transmission involves us in a process of communication by which distinct parties in the transaction engage in a mutual conversation. The culture, social needs, personal needs and religious needs of the interlocutors will be the point of inculturation and incarnation of the Good News today.[67]

In these contexts the call is for renewed vigour and commitment, for seeking to develop new techniques and methods and to find new ways of communicating the Gospel.

New ardour: The priority for the work of the Church is the Gospel, being formed in the Gospel in such a way that Christians feel impelled to communicate and share the good news they have received. The American bishops produced a National Strategy for Evangelisation. In this they declared their intent:

> I. To bring about in all Catholics such an enthusiasm for their faith that in living their faith in Jesus, they freely share it with others.
>
> II. To invite all people in the United States, whatever their social or cultural background, to hear the message of salvation in Jesus Christ, so they may come to join us in the fullness of the Catholic faith.
>
> III. To foster gospel values in our society, promoting the

---

[66] See for instance Leonardo Boff, *New Evangelization: Good News to the Poor* (Orbis, Maryknoll NY, 1991).

[67] We will examine some specific implications of this for England and Wales in the section on *Contextualisation* below, p. 68.

dignity of the human person, the importance of the family, and the common good of society, so that our nation may continue to be transformed by the saving power of Jesus Christ.[68]

While our context is not identical to the American one, nonetheless a parallel statement could find wide acceptance in England and Wales. Part of the newness of New Evangelisation is to promote an enthusiasm for the faith amongst believers which communicates itself to the world and people in the world.

New methods: Each age of evangelisation has found appropriate techniques with which to express and share the Gospel. As people ask new questions, new ways of engaging with their faith journey must be found. New circumstances demand new forms of evangelisation. This may well force us into uncomfortable areas. We may have to take risks with things which prove imperfect or unproductive. We do have to discover how the Good News of Jesus, the Good News which is Jesus, can be shared today. This will mean being open to international and ecumenical insights and to encouraging the use of imagination and creativity in our own communities. The gifts of all Christians should be used to contribute to the tasks of evangelisation.

New means of communication: The least known decree of the Second Vatican Council probably remains *Inter Mirifica*. Yet the means of social communication are fundamental to evangelisation. Indeed since 1963 these have multiplied. Printed publications, radio and television broadcasts, cinema, video, DVD and other multimedia avenues, internet and other electronic forms of communications have made our time an age in which information can be communicated with great ease but into a market place over-filled with an excess of information. The conciliar document referred to the modern media as a 'great

---

[68] *Go and Make Disciples: A National Plan and Strategy for Catholic Evangelisation* quoted by Bishop William Houck in the introduction to Ralph Martin and Peter Williamson (ed.), *John Paul II and the New Evangelisation* (Ignatius Press, San Francisco, 1995), p. 19f.

round table'.[69] More recent thinking has opened them up as
areopagi - places where we can engage with those outside the
Church and enable people to hear that of their lives which offers
worship to the unknown God.

> The first Areopagus of the modern age is the *world of
> communications*, which is unifying humanity and turning it into
> what is known as a 'global village'. The means of social
> communication have become so important as to be for many the
> chief means of information and education, of guidance and
> inspiration in their behavior as individuals, families and within
> society at large. In particular, the younger generation is growing
> up in a world conditioned by the mass media. To some degree
> perhaps this Areopagus has been neglected. Generally,
> preference has been given to other means of preaching the
> Gospel and of Christian education, while the mass media are
> left to the initiative of individuals or small groups and enter into
> pastoral planning only in a secondary way. Involvement in the
> mass media, however, is not meant merely to strengthen the
> preaching of the Gospel. There is a deeper reality involved here:
> since the very evangelization of modern culture depends to a
> great extent on the influence of the media, it is not enough to use
> the media simply to spread the Christian message and the
> Church's authentic teaching. It is also necessary to integrate that
> message into the 'new culture' created by modern
> communications. This is a complex issue, since the 'new culture'
> originates not just from whatever content is eventually
> expressed, but from the very fact that there exist new ways of
> communicating, with new languages, new techniques and a
> new psychology.[70]

New Evangelisation grows out of the theological vision of
the Pontiff. Although it is invidious to summarise the rich,
nuanced and multi-layered thought of Pope John Paul II we can
see three layers of particular relevance to our purposes: the

[69] *Inter Mirifica* 19.
[70] *Redemptoris Missio* 37 (c).

significance of the global, the ecclesial and the personal. All of these shape the thrust of and the newness of 'New Evangelisation'.

A foundation stone of the thinking of the present Pontiff has been the global, indeed cosmic, significance of the incarnation. The mystery of the Word made flesh reveals the mystery of humanity.[71] This conciliar insight (with which Bishop Karol Wojtyla was actively involved[72]) lies at the heart of the first encyclical of John Paul II:

> Man as 'willed' by God, as 'chosen' by him from eternity and called, destined for grace and glory - this is 'each' man, 'the most concrete' man, the most real; this is man in all the fullness of the mystery in which he has become a sharer in Jesus Christ, the mystery in which each one of the four thousand million human beings on our planet has become a sharer from the moment he is conceived beneath the heart of his mother.[73]

The Gospel is therefore constitutive of all people and a profound dignity is ascribed to the human condition through Christ. This reality of the human person is lessened by sin and needs to come to completion through grace, yet it remains a universal state of being. Through the incarnation God's self-sending mission of love has entered into every sphere of humanity both judging each person, arousing in him or her a yearning for completeness and opening everyone up to the potential of redemption.[74] The transformation that accepting the Gospel brings is the coming to awareness of one's status before God. One is loved: one is already touched by the incarnation. The evangelising mission of the Church is to make that truth explicit.

---

[71] *Gaudium et Spes* 22.

[72] Herbert Vorgrimler, *Commentary on the documents of Vatican II* vol. 5 (Burns and Oates/Herder and Herder, London and New York, 1969), pp. 38, 44, 50, 63.

[73] *Redemptor Hominis* (1979) 39.

[74] Cf. *Redemptoris Missio* 3.

The dominant Catholic ecclesiology of recent times may be seen as a theology of *communio* which encompasses both unity and mutuality. This *communio* has several inter-penetrating aspects: it is rooted in the Divine Communion of the Trinity; It is mediated through sacramental communion (communion in holy things); it is incarnated in the relationships that Christians have with one another (communion of sanctified people); *communio* has a special expression in the relationships between the local Churches and the one worldwide Church, not least in terms of the relationship between the Pope and local bishops - and also in the network of relationships with other ecclesial realities and ecumenical partners; it expresses itself in charity and self-giving, which are both theological principles and practical demands. Charity is particularly seen in solidarity with the poorest and most needy; *communio* is also missionary in that the Church is called to be a sacrament of communion to the world:

> the Church is not a reality closed in on herself. Rather, she is permanently open to missionary and ecumenical endeavour, for she is sent to the world to announce and witness, to make present and spread the mystery of communion which is essential to her, and to gather all people and all things into Christ, so as to be for all an 'inseparable sacrament of unity'.[75]

In alliance with these global and ecclesial concerns there has also been a strong restatement of the importance of the personal element of faith. Although the previous two aspects clearly move us onto a different canvas from the classic evangelical emphasis on 'knowing Jesus as your personal Lord and Saviour', yet there is some common ground here. Within the mystery of being human revealed by the incarnation of the Divine Son and the community of faith which is the Church,

---

[75] Congregation for the Doctrine of the Faith, Letter to the Bishops of the Catholic Church on Some Aspects of the Church Understood as Communion, *Communionis Notio* (28 May 1992), 4. Cf. Karol Wojtyla, *Sources of Renewal* (Collins, London, 1980), pp. 112-154 and 367-418.

each man, woman and child must grow into a faith which is a personal relationship with God in Christ. Perhaps the most moving recent meditation upon this has again been in *Novo Millennio Ineunte* and its discussion built around contemplating the 'face of Jesus':

> We are certainly not seduced by the naive expectation that, faced with the great challenges of our time, we shall find some magic formula. No, we shall not be saved by a formula but by a Person, and the assurance which he gives us: *I am with you!*
>
> It is not therefore a matter of inventing a 'new programme'. The programme already exists: it is the plan found in the Gospel and in the living Tradition, it is the same as ever. Ultimately, it has its centre in Christ himself, who is to be known, loved and imitated, so that in him we may live the life of the Trinity, and with him transform history until its fulfilment in the heavenly Jerusalem. This is a programme which does not change with shifts of times and cultures, even though it takes account of time and culture for the sake of true dialogue and effective communication. This programme for all times is our programme for the Third Millennium.[76]

John Paul II has strongly seen 'New Evangelisation' as the challenge of our times to the Church.

> God is opening before the Church the horizons of a humanity more fully prepared for the sowing of the Gospel. I sense that the moment has come to commit all of the Church's energies to a new evangelization and to the mission *ad gentes*. No believer in Christ, no institution of the Church can avoid this supreme duty: to proclaim Christ to all peoples.[77]

This is a universal calling of the Church - and a universal call to all in the Church. It is the place where the Pope has called for

[76] *Novo Millennio Ineunte* 29. This may be considered the climax of the meditation on 'A Face to Contemplate' in *Novo Millennio Ineunte* 16-28.

[77] *Redemptoris Missio* 3.

all the Church's energies to be committed. The ministers of the 'New Evangelisation' are all believers in Christ and all Church institutions. One of the most exciting, of several exciting aspects, of living in this time of 'New Evangelisation' is for every Christian to discern and enact her or his own contribution to this vital duty. All ecclesial realities: parishes, communities, movements, lay associations, individual Christians in whatever state of life, are called to be evangelisers.

The identity of the evangelisers

As we shall consider below, God is a missionary God: evangelisation happens because of the sending of the divine Son and the Holy Spirit. Indeed evangelisation comes from Christ and the Holy Spirit is the primary evangeliser. The Twelve were evangelised themselves before being commissioned as evangelisers by Christ and in the power of the Spirit. Thus evangelisation is also an expression of ministry in the Church. While some may have particular gifts and special ministry in this field, all are called to contribute. Those who have been evangelised become evangelisers:

> the man who has been evangelized becomes himself an evangelizer. This is the proof, the test of the genuineness of his own conversion. It is inconceivable that a man who has received the word and surrendered himself to the kingdom should not himself become a witness and proclaimer of the truth.[78]

There is an important issue here of who are the evangelisers. It is not enough to define a few specialists as evangelisers - although some specialist ministries may be appropriately recognised and supported. All Christ's faithful must contribute to this fundamental being and activity of the Church. Bishops

---

[78] *Evangelii Nuntiandi* 24.

are evangelisers in the Church.[79] The apostolic ministry of priests commits them to the work of evangelisation.[80] Many communities, societies, congregations and movements have evangelisation at the heart of their constitutions and charism. Above all it must be stressed that the identity of baptised Christians as the Royal Priesthood orders every member of the Church to the work of proclaiming and enacting the Gospel. In the words of the Council:

> Since the whole Church is missionary, and the work of evangelization the fundamental task of the people of God, this sacred Synod invites all to undertake a profound interior renewal so that being vitally conscious of their responsibility for the spread of the Gospel they might play their part in missionary work among the nations.

> As members of the living Christ, incorporated into him and made like him by baptism, confirmation and the Eucharist, all the faithful have an obligation to collaborate in the expansion and spread of his Body, so that they might bring it to fullness as soon as possible (cf. Ephesians 4:13).

I feel in order to evangelise outside the Church, many parishes still need to be 'evangelised' themselves. Priests and people together need to explore and understand what is meant by collaborative ministry. Some Catholics still come to Mass because they fear the penalty of mortal sin - they need to know that God loves them and hopefully will respond with a deeper understanding and commitment to what is offered by the Catholic Church; then they will want 'to share' their faith with others.

Respondent to general survey

---

[79] See Vatican II, *Christus Dominus* 12, and the *Instrumentum Laboris* of the Synod of Bishops 10th Ordinary General Assembly, 'The Bishop: Servant of the Gospel of Jesus Christ for the Hope of the World' June 2001, and the reflections of Bishop Malcolm McMahon OP in *Catholic Gazette*, September, October, November 2001.

[80] See Pope John Paul II, *Pastores Dabo Vobis* (1992) 2, 6-7.

So all the children of the Church should have a lively consciousness of their own responsibility for the world, they should foster within themselves a truly Catholic spirit, they should spend themselves in the work of the Gospel.[81]

While affirming the necessity and importance of bishops, priests, deacons and religious as evangelisers, we must also emphasise that evangelisation is the calling and work of all Christ's faithful people. As the *Code of Canon Law* makes clear:

Canon 210. All Christ's faithful, each according to his or her own condition, must make a wholehearted effort to lead a holy life, and to promote the growth of the Church and its continual sanctification.

Canon 211. All Christ's faithful have the obligation and right to strive so that the divine message of salvation may more and more reach all people of all times and all places.

Canon 225. §1. Since the laity like all the Christian faithful are deputed by God to the apostolate through their baptism and confirmation, they are therefore bound by the general obligations and enjoy the general right to work as individuals or in associations so that the divine message of salvation becomes known and accepted by all persons throughout the world; this obligation has a greater impelling force in those circumstances in which people can hear the gospel and know Christ only through lay persons.

The 'coal face' of evangelisation is located in families and schools, workplaces and neighbourhoods. The Gospel takes root in Christian women and men and children who become agents of its transmission, growth and fruition in the world.

Christian community both serves the needs of Christians and supports them and demands full participation of all Christians in the web of service which constitutes the Church

---

[81] *Ad Gentes* 35-36. See *Evangelii Nuntiandi* 70-73 and Pope John Paul II, *Christifideles Laici* (1988) 2 (and indeed this is the thrust of the entirety of this Apostolic Exhortation).

and through which the Church reaches out into the world. All Christians are called to participate in ways within their grasp in evangelisation. Appropriate formation for all members of the Church is therefore called for. The first step of this is to enable people to realise that they are both evangelised and responsible actors in evangelisation.

The document *The Sign We Give* has been a signal attempt by the Church in these nations to promote collaborative ministry. The communion we seek to model is both a goal and a means of evangelisation.

> The theme of communion has also given rise to a renewed and integrated theology of mission. It overcomes any separation between Church and world by proposing that the whole Church is to be intimately concerned with the world and deeply involved in its life precisely by living communion as fully as possible. The Church carries out its mission by living its own life, and this is the eternal way in which the gospel is proclaimed. As the Church lives communion, all people and all creation are drawn towards unity and community. This is the full meaning of collaborative ministry; not simply to renew the life of the Church, but to enable the Church to be part of transforming the world.[82]

The proper mutual working together of all members of the Church is therefore the necessary condition of evangelisation and a fruit of evangelisation.

Orientations in understanding evangelisation

The above discussion suggests several orientations in understanding evangelisation:

1. The **source of evangelisation** is the encounter of the mystery of God in Christ with the world and the ongoing

[82] Bishops' Conference of England and Wales, *The Sign We Give* (Matthew James Publishing, Chelmsford, 1995), p. 13.

activity of the Holy Spirit. It is this work of the triune God which brings Good News to people and brings about Good News for people; it establishes and renews the Church and commissions and empowers the Church to share Good News with others.

2. The **nature of evangelisation** is a complex and dynamic process which integrates the proclamation and enactment of the Good News of the kingdom and the salvation offered in God's universal grace both of which are incarnate in the person of Christ Jesus. The controlling frame of evangelisation is the Gospel. Mission creates a frame of meaning dependent on sending and being sent; evangelisation creates a frame of meaning around the Gospel. As such the terms are intimately connected and overlap but are not simple synonyms. For the Church evangelisation brings the Gospel into all areas of her being and doing. It involves proclamation and dialogue, word and sacrament, wordless and spoken witness, life and celebration, personal conversion, ecclesial renewal and social transformation.

3. The **context of evangelisation** demands that the Church take seriously the contemporary situations in service of the Gospel. The practical outworking of the call to evangelisation will shape the Church's actions as she engages with the needs of men and women today in their varying and fragmented contexts. All within the Church have a duty to contribute to the proclamation and enactment of the Gospel.

> Be confident, upbeat, bold in the Good News we proclaim. The product we're offering is the best in the world
> *Respondent to PP survey*

Evangelisation does therefore include all activities in which the Gospel is encountered and furthered. This is both what happens to the Church when she allows the Gospel to renew her and when the Church shares the Gospel she has received with others. The Church both transmits this Gospel and discovers it in the world. An essential element of evangelisation is the conscious aim of presenting the Gospel to those beyond the Church in order to form new Christians. However, evangelisation is the encounter of the Gospel with all people, including those within the Church. The spread of the Gospel is a dynamic force which converts people, transforms society and renews the Church. Personal life and lifestyles, values and morality, cultures and societies are all transfigured by the active Good News of God in Christ.

Evangelisation, as the spread of the Gospel, includes all the processes of forming new Christians as well as the deliberate enactment of the Good News in such things as the promotion of Justice and Peace. There is an integral whole by which words and action complete each other. However, the Church needs to avoid diluting evangelisation by equating it with everything that the Church does. Evangelisation is wide and comprehensive, but this may make it so wide as to be meaningless or to legitimate the ignoring of essential components. Evangelisation must contain a commitment to form disciples, to build the Church and to bring good news to the poor and liberty to captives. All that the Church does affects and may even effect evangelisation but evangelisation must remain the urgent necessity to proclaim and enact the Good News of God in Christ. An essential location of evangelisation must be the Church reaching out beyond the Church.

From definition to practicalities:
Some Imaginary Catholic communities

The Parish of Our Lady of Pastoral Care:

• Parish energies go into supporting Christians and Christian families.
• Serving the liturgical and pastoral needs of parishioners, including caring for wounded and hurt people, takes up most of the time of the parish clergy and lay workers.
• The Catholic school is a major activity which serves the Catholic community.

The Oscar Romero Basic Community:

• The group is formed of 'conscientised' individuals profoundly committed to resisting injustice.
• Social and political issues dominate discussion and activities.
• Common ground is made with radical groups outside the Church.

The Proclamation Prayer Group:

• This loose group is eager to convince others of the Lordship of Jesus Christ.
• Individual conversions and apologetics form the focus of their activities.
• Common cause is often made with Evangelical and Charismatic groups.

None of the above exist beyond these writers' minds. (If by accident the title of any actual community has been stumbled upon then we apologise and withdraw the description unreservedly.) Yet we suspect they will be recognisable. None represents the perfect evangelising community but evangelisation is happening in all of them.

To use negative clichés, the first could be castigated for being concerned with maintenance more than mission, the second with reducing Christianity to secular humanism, and the last with being too heavenly minded to be of any earthly use. However, such condemnatory opinions disguise the real value present in each of the caricatures. The first emphasises *koinonia*, the second *diakonia*, and the last *kerygma*. All these aspects of community/communion, service and proclamation contribute to evangelisation. The challenge is to integrate all these aspects in genuine communities which care for each other, care for the world and care for the spiritual and other needs of those outside their visible community. The above may represent less poles in a fragmented approach to mission than factors in a unified response to the Good News received by the Church in Jesus Christ.

3. Missio Dei

Recent Catholic, ecumenical and Evangelical theology of mission has converged under the sometimes confusing label of *Missio Dei*. By this we understand the following necessary components:

- Mission flows from the life of the Trinity.
- Mission is God's work gathering all things to himself in Christ.
- The Holy Spirit is the primary evangelist.
- The goal of mission is not the Church *per se* but the kingdom of God.
- The Church is the sacrament of the kingdom.

The central thrust of the mission theology of Vatican II is to locate what the Church does in the activity of the Triune God.

The pilgrim Church is missionary by her very nature, since it is from the mission of the Son and the mission of the Holy Spirit that she draws her origin, in accordance with the decree of God the Father. This decree, however, flows from the 'fount-like love' or charity of God the Father who, being the 'principle without principle' from whom the Son is begotten and the Holy Spirit proceeds through the Son, freely creating us on account of His surpassing and merciful kindness and graciously calling us moreover to share with Him His life and His glory, has generously poured out, and does not cease to pour out still, His divine goodness. Thus He who created all things may at last be 'all in all' (1 Corinthians 15:28), bringing about at one and the same time His own glory and our happiness. But it pleased God to call men to share His life, not just singly, apart from any mutual bond, but rather to mould them into a people in which His sons, once scattered abroad, might be gathered together (cf. John 11:52).[83]

---

[83] *Ad Gentes* 2.

The love of the Father is articulated in the Son and through the Holy Spirit. The Church's mission is not just a consequence of the sending of Christ but a continuation of the mission of Christ. The Church is enabled and impelled in this by the Holy Spirit. As such we must declare the great works of God, participate in God's plan for the universe and co-operate in the building up of the kingdom of God as we look towards the consummation of all things in Christ. The source, power and destiny of the mission of the Church is dependent upon the mission of God. The mission of the Church is to take part in the mission of God. However, the Church is not the goal of that mission, but a servant of it.

Missio Dei relocates the primary weight of the concept of mission away from Church structures and the practical organisation of territories and portions of the people of God to God. The essence of mission is to be found in the love of God the Father reaching out through the Son and the Holy Spirit. There is an almost *gestalt* shift here from focus upon 'missions' (buildings and personnel in lands where the Church is yet to be fully established) towards 'mission' (God's loving extension of himself which includes the sending of the Church).[84] Mission is God reaching out to the world to draw all people to himself. The mission of the Church is the continuation of the mission of Christ empowered by the mission of the Holy Spirit. Christian mission becomes seen as the participation of the Church in the activity of the Holy Trinity. Whereas the language of mission in previous generations was commonly military (crusade, soldiers of Christ, conquest, winning souls etc.) the images and actions growing from a Trinitarian theology of *missio Dei* are relational (love, dialogue, sharing, community, solidarity, integral human development etc.).[85]

[84] Indeed this shift may be traced from the 1970s in the choice of language in Catholicism by which talk of missions has largely been replaced by the concept of evangelisation. See the discussion above.

[85] See Robert J. Schreiter, 'Changes in Roman Catholic Attitudes toward Proselytism and Mission' in James A. Scherer and Stephen B. Bevans, *New Directions in Mission and Evangelization 2: Theological Foundations* (Orbis, Maryknoll NY, 1994), p. 117, and Donal Dorr, *Mission in Today's World* (Columba, Dublin, 2000), p. 186f.

The purpose of the *missio Dei* is the inauguration, building up and eventual consummation of the kingdom of God. It is less the setting up and extension of the Church than understanding why the Church was set up. As such 'mission' is not a specialist activity by specialist ministers in particular areas but the root identity of the

> I am very concerned that evangelisation should be seen as the building of God's reign in the world and not the bringing of people into the Church (though this must be done too).
> *Respondent in PP survey*

entire Church in all places and the work of all Christians. It is what God is doing, what God is doing for us, what God is doing through us and how we respond to God. Mission is not the colonial expansion of the Church; it is the Church participating in God's work.

Because God is love he acts out of love: because the Church is formed by the calling of this loving God, she must act out of love for God and those God loves. The dynamic of the mission of the Church is formed by how God is and what God does.[86] Because God's grace has been showered on us we are called to share the benefits we have received with others. Because our lives are transformed then we must transform the world. God's

---

[86] Cf. Yves Conger OP, 'Die Theologie, die der Missionstätigkeit zugrunde liegt, ist nicht allein im allgemeinen Sinne einer epistemologischen Lokalisierung theologisch - das heißt, einfach weil es hier um eine Abhandlung geht, deren Prinzipien oder Postulate aus dem Glauben stammen. Sie ist theologisch durch ihren Inhalt der im strengsten Sinne eine Abhandlung über Gott ist, ja selbst in jenem ganz speziellen Sinne, in dem the griechischen Väter, namentlich die Kappadozier, zwischen der "Theologie" (Gott in sich selbst betrachtet; der Dreifaltige und Eine; die Schöpfung) und der "Œkonomie" (die Austeilung der Gnade und vor allem die Menschwerdung) unterscheiden. Der Text will zeigen, wie die Dynamik, durch welche die Kirche sich selbst in der Welt ausbreitet, über einen institutionellen Akt und einen Auftrag hinaus, nicht nur mit der Sendung der zweiten und dritten Person der Heiligen Dreifaltigkeit verlnüpft ist sondern auch mit dem innersten und, wenn man so sagen kann, dem innergöttlichen Leben des lebendigen Gottes selbst.' In Johannes Schütte, *Mission nach dem Konzil* (Matthias Grünewold Verlag, Mainz, 1967), p. 134f.

love for the world compels us to follow his mission and to follow the Divine Son, the Holy Spirit and the grace of God into the world. The love of God transforms persons, societies and history, the Church is witness to and instrument of that transformation.

God's purpose in reaching out is to gather in. The Holy Trinity is not just the source of the Church's mission but her goal. *Missio Dei* involves both the movement of God towards humanity and the movement of humanity towards God.[87]

> The ultimate purpose of mission is to enable people to share in the communion which exists between the Father and the Son.[88]

The Church is part of God's gathering of all things to himself. The Church is a partner in this gathering in of all things.

> And so the time for missionary activity extends between the first coming of the Lord and the second, in which latter the Church will be gathered from the four winds like a harvest into the kingdom of God. For the Gospel must be preached to all nations before the Lord shall come (cf. Mark 13:10).
>
> Missionary activity is nothing else and nothing less than an epiphany, or a manifesting of God's decree, and its fulfilment in the world and in world history, in the course of which God, by means of mission, manifestly works out the history of salvation. By the preaching of the word and by the celebration of the sacraments, the centre and summit of which is the most holy

---

[87] Cf. Cardinal Zoa, 'La missione ha la sua fonte prima nella missione del Verbo e dello Spirito. E'questa missione che continua nella Chiesa e per mezzo della Chiesa, che ne è lo strumento. Si tratta d'un unico movimento che viene della Trinita e va verso la Trinita e che attraversa il monde e la storia. La missione conte, per i christiani, as entere in questo movimento che ha mosso il Verbo verso gli uomini, als fine de mouvere gli uomini verso il Padre, ed a cooperare con lo Spirito Santo che, come un flume d'aqua viva, cerca di sollevare la nostra pesante umanità per innalzarla verso ii Padre.' Quoted by Anne Marie Aagaard, '*Missio Dei* in katolischer Sicht: Missiontheologische Tendenzen', *Evangelische Theologie* 5 (September/October 1974), p. 423.

[88] *Redemptoris Missio* 24.

Eucharist, He brings about the presence of Christ, the author of salvation. But whatever truth and grace are to be found among the nations, as a sort of secret presence of God, He frees from all taint of evil and restores to Christ its maker, who overthrows the devil's domain and wards off the manifold malice of vice. And so, whatever good is found to be sown in the hearts and minds of men, or in the rites and cultures peculiar to various peoples, not only is not lost, but is healed, uplifted, and perfected for the glory of God, the shame of the demon, and the bliss of men. Thus, missionary activity tends toward eschatological fullness.[89]

There is a necessary Trinitarian-Christocentricity[90] to mission and the ultimate purpose of mission. The realisation of God's plan of salvation, when all will be brought together in Christ (cf. Ephesians 1:3-14), is both the calling of the Church and the hope to be shared with others. The grace of God in Christ is both to be preached by the Church and celebrated in her sacraments. However, this same grace is to be found 'among the nations'. The Church discovers (uncovers) truth and grace as 'a sort of secret presence of God'. Dialogue with others is part of this process of uncovering more and more of the eschatalogical fullness in Christ. Such fullness is a promise to the Church, not an absolute possession. The pilgrim Church is *en route* to that fullness and is thus constantly encountering more and more of the definitive revelation of God in Christ (cf. Ephesians 3:16-19). The mission of the Church is to co-operate in the building up of this fullness (Ephesians 4:11-13).

The Holy Spirit is the pledge of this eschatalogical fullness. More than this the Spirit is the communicator and the one who empowers the mission which seeks out this goal. The Spirit is active in God's reaching out to humanity and in the human response. It is the Spirit which draws all things to their consummation and fulfilment in God.

---

[89] *Ad Gentes* 9.
[90] Cf. *General Directory for Catechesis* 99-100.

It must be said that the Holy Spirit is the principal agent of evangelization: it is He who impels each individual to proclaim the Gospel, and it is He who in the depths of consciences causes the word of salvation to be accepted and understood. But it can equally be said that He is the goal of evangelization: He alone stirs up the new creation, the new humanity of which evangelization is to be the result, with that unity in variety which evangelization wishes to achieve within the Christian community. Through the Holy Spirit the Gospel penetrates to the heart of the world, for it is He who causes people to discern the signs of the times - signs willed by God - which evangelization reveals and puts to use within history.[91]

Although present in a special way in the Church, the Holy Spirit is also universal, present to and active among all people. Individuals, society and history are touched by the Holy Spirit. 'The Spirit, therefore, is at the very source of humanity's existential and religious questioning'.[92] The Holy Spirit sows seeds of the Gospel, and actively draws all men and women into the kingdom of God.

Thus the Spirit, who 'blows where he wills' (cf. John 3:8), who 'was already at work in the world before Christ was glorified,' and who 'has filled the world, ... holds all things together [and] knows what is said' (Wisdom 1:7), leads us to broaden our vision in order to ponder his activity in every time and place. ... This is the same Spirit who was at work in the Incarnation and in the life, death and resurrection of Jesus, and who is at work in the Church. He is therefore not an alternative to Christ, nor does he fill a sort of void which is sometimes suggested as existing between Christ and the *Logos*. Whatever the Spirit brings about in human hearts and in the history of peoples, in cultures and religions, serves as a preparation for the Gospel and can only be understood in reference to Christ, the Word who took flesh by

---

[91] *Evangelii Nuntiandi* 75.
[92] *Redemptoris Missio* 28.

the power of the Spirit 'so that as perfectly human he would save all human beings and sum up all things'.[93]

The Holy Spirit has been active throughout in salvation history; since creation, through the exodus, rise of kingship, in the exile and return from exile, in the incarnation of the Word and the birth and growth of the Church. It is the same Spirit that remains active today leading all things to their consummation in Christ. The 'hidden, mysterious and invisible mission of the Spirit'[94] unites the mission of Christ and the mission of the Church. In terms of *missio Dei*, the Holy Spirit is our most immediate encounter with the active love of God in our hearts, in our Church and in our world.

The Church is not the goal of mission; the purpose of the *missio Dei* is the kingdom of God. The Church serves the kingdom. The kingdom comes through the work of Christ. It is God's reigning over all creation in a divine community of brothers and sisters. The kingdom is the overarching concept that contains the Church and her mission.

> MISSION is in the first place mission of God (*Missio Dei*) whose aim is the coming of his Kingdom. When we pray for the coming of God's Kingdom, we pray and work not so much for the expansion of the Church or for unity among Christians, but rather for 'a redeemed, a healed, a mended creation' ... on a personal, communal and cosmic level.[95]

This is not the place to develop further the rich concept of the kingdom of God except to note several dialectics: the kingdom is inaugurated but not yet consummated; the kingdom is before,

---

[93] *Redemptoris Missio* 29.

[94] Tommaso Fedenci, 'Pneumatological Foundation of Mission' in Karotemprel, *Following Christ in Mission*, p. 73.

[95] Frans J. Verstraelen, 'World Mission: towards a Common Missiology' in *Mission Studies* 1 (1984), p. 35. Verstraelen is a Catholic scholar working in an ecumenical institute and this paper consciously seeks common ground between current understandings of mission across Christian traditions.

within, upon and close to all people; the kingdom transforms the person, his or her relationships, human society and the entirety of creation. A theology of mission which takes the kingdom of God as its heart will seek to bring that transformation into all the dimensions of humanity and indeed into the integrity of the non-human world.[96]

> The kingdom of God is meant for all humankind, and all people are called to become members of it. To emphasize this fact, Jesus drew especially near to those on the margins of society, and showed them special favor in announcing the Good News. At the beginning of his ministry he proclaimed that he was 'anointed ... to preach good news to the poor' (Luke 4:18). To all who are victims of rejection and contempt Jesus declares: 'Blessed are you poor' (Luke 6:20). What is more, he enables such individuals to experience liberation even now, by being close to them, going to eat in their homes (cf. Luke 5:30; 15:2), treating them as equals and friends (cf. Luke 7:34), and making them feel loved by God, thus revealing his tender care for the needy and for sinners (cf. Luke 15:1-32). The liberation and salvation brought by the kingdom of God come to the human person both in his physical and spiritual dimensions. ...
>
> The kingdom aims at transforming human relationships; it grows gradually as people slowly learn to love, forgive and serve one another. Jesus sums up the whole Law, focusing it on the commandment of love. ... The kingdom's nature, therefore, is one of communion among all human beings - with one another and with God.

---

[96] See Michael Amadloss SJ, 'The Church as Servant of the Coming Kingdom', and Barbara Hendricks MM, 'Mission in Service of God's Reign', both in Gerald H. Anderson, James M. Phillips and Robert T. Coote (ed.), *Mission in the 1990s* (Eerdmans, Grand Rapids, 1991), p. 14f. and p. 26f. respectively. On the issues of Justice, Peace and the Integrity of Creation see *The Assisi Declarations* (Century Hutchinson/WWF UK, London, 1987). Pope John Paul II, Message for World Peace Day, 1 January 1990, *The Ecological Crisis: a common responsibility*. Much of the fruits of recent discussion in the World Council of Churches can be accessed at {www.wcc-coe.org/wcc/what/jpc/ecology.html}.

The kingdom is the concern of everyone: individuals, society, and the world. Working for the kingdom means acknowledging and promoting God's activity, which is present in human history and transforms it. Building the kingdom means working for liberation from evil in all its forms. In a word, the kingdom of God is the manifestation and the realization of God's plan of salvation in all its fullness.[97]

Kingdom-centred mission relocates the primary purposes of mission away from Church expansion. This is not to say that numerical increase in Church membership does not help the growth of the kingdom (see below) but that the goal of Church growth is the transformation of the world to be closer to the kingdom of God, or, better, to move towards the consummation of the kingdom.

Although the kingdom is central, this does not make the Church unnecessary or peripheral. The Church is a privileged agency in the growth of the kingdom and the growth of the Church is part of God's plan. The kingdom is overarching, but the Church is necessarily involved with the kingdom.

Although God's Mission is realized in ways and manners which are beyond the Church, the Church as the community commissioned by Christ, is the primary participant in the *Missio Dei* for its historical, visible realization and continuation.[98]

The secularised kingdom which ecumenical discussion of the *missio Dei* sometimes seemed to promote is rejected by the present Pontiff.

There are also conceptions which deliberately emphasize the kingdom and which describe themselves as 'kingdom centered.' They stress the image of a Church which is not concerned about herself, but which is totally concerned with bearing witness to

---

[97] *Redemptoris Missio* 14-15.
[98] Verstraelen, p. 36.

and serving the kingdom. It is a 'Church for others' just as Christ is the 'man for others.' The Church's task is described as though it had to proceed in two directions: on the one hand promoting such 'values of the kingdom' as peace, justice, freedom, brotherhood, etc., while on the other hand fostering dialogue between peoples, cultures and religions, so that through a mutual enrichment they might help the world to be renewed and to journey ever closer toward the kingdom.

Together with positive aspects, these conceptions often reveal negative aspects as well. First, they are silent about Christ: the kingdom of which they speak is 'theocentrically' based, since, according to them, Christ cannot be understood by those who lack Christian faith, whereas different peoples, cultures and religions are capable of finding common ground in the one divine reality, by whatever name it is called. For the same reason they put great stress on the mystery of creation, which is reflected in the diversity of cultures and beliefs, but they keep silent about the mystery of redemption. Furthermore, the kingdom, as they understand it, ends up either leaving very little room for the Church or undervaluing the Church in reaction to a presumed 'ecclesiocentrism' of the past, and because they consider the Church herself only a sign, for that matter a sign not without ambiguity.

This is not the kingdom of God as we know it from Revelation. The kingdom cannot be detached either from Christ or from the Church.[99]

The Church 'is not an end unto herself',[100] she is ordered to the kingdom of God. However, the Church is united to the kingdom. Church and kingdom are not coterminous but they are intimately related. 'The kingdom cannot be detached either from Christ or from the Church.' The Church is a sacrament of the communion with God and unity among all people that we

[99] *Redemptoris Missio* 17-18.
[100] *Redemptoris Missio* 18.

recognise as the kingdom of God.[101] The Church is established by Christ to be the seed and sign of the kingdom.[102] There is an anticipation in the Church of the kingdom, but the fullness of the kingdom is yet to come. However, the Church already incarnates (or at least should incarnate) aspects of the kingdom: universality and constancy, the place of offering the sacrifice of thanks and praise, the glorification of God in word and deed, the obedience to God's sovereignty, the living out of love, justice and peace.[103] 'In the Church we find the visible manifestation of the project that God is silently carrying out in the world.'[104]

The ideas associated with *missio Dei* can seem so diverse as to be confusing. However, they do shape a priority for understanding the mission of the Church today. The mission of God transcends, establishes and will fulfil the mission of the Church. God is the great missionary. Mission grows out of the nature of God to reach out in love that all may be drawn into his love. This is fundamentally Trinitarian. It relates Creator to his creation and links the experience of divine transcendence with the experience of divine immanence. The sending of the Son and Holy Spirit establish the second and third persons of the Trinity as primary evangelisers. The Church is formed by these missions and is formed as a missionary body because of the nature of the God who forms her. The Church is part of the nexus whereby God relates with his world and his people. The

[101] Cf. Vatican II, *Lumen Gentium* 1, and 'The Church, inasmuch as she is one and unique, is as a sacrament a sign and instrument of unity and of reconciliation, of peace among men, nations, classes and peoples.' Extraordinary Synod of Bishops 1985, Final Relatio, *L'Osservatore Romano (English Weekly Edition)*, 16 December 1985, p. 7.

[102] Cf. *Lumen Gentium* 5.

[103] Cf. The Preface for Christ the King: 'As King he claims dominion over all creation, that he may present to you, his almighty Father, an eternal and universal kingdom: a kingdom of truth and life, a kingdom of holiness and grace, a kingdom of justice, love and peace.'

[104] Third General Conference of Latin American Bishops, Puebla, *Evangelization at Present and in the Future of Latin America* quoted by Paul Vadakupadan SDB, 'Ecclessiological Foundation of Mission' in Karotemprel, *Following Christ in Mission*, p. 77.

Church in mission participates in the mission of God. The ultimate goal of the mission of God is the consummation of all things in Christ. One essential image of this is the kingdom of God which asserts the sovereignty of God in all the dimensions of human life, human society and cultures and the entirety of the cosmos. The Church is the sacrament of this kingly reign of God and a beacon of the divine communion to the world.

4. Contextualisation

The dynamic of mission always implies a threefold continuum of sending: the sender (God the Father, the Holy Trinity), the sent (Christ, the Holy Spirit, the Church), and those they are sent to (people and the world). This last gives a special weight to the experiences and forces which situate people in the world. Recent reflection has highlighted the importance of cultural and material questions in the mission of the Church. One of the recurring themes of contemporary theology of mission is the need to address the contexts that people are situated in.[105] Mission may come from God, the Church may participate in it, but it has a focus in those to whom the Church is sent. The needs, perceptions, cultures and language games of those outside the Church are therefore addressed and engaged with by evangelisation.

This includes the reality of social change. It may be that this social change will call for change in the Church, the Church being prepared to grow into the new culture that is being formed or it may be that the Church should be a counter-cultural sign revealing and resisting dehumanising social changes. Sometimes social change is to be welcomed and supported as furthering the kingdom of God; sometimes change can be inimical to the kingdom. There is an evangelising task of discernment in seeing which social changes are to be affirmed, which are to be

> My own view at present is that the future lies in inspiring our young people to shape the world. The radical changes in society and the view of our responsibility for the whole world has forced us into a reappraisal of how the Church operates. While this can be disconcerting it also pushes us into a need to look honestly and directly at our fundamental relationships with God and with each other, following the clear values lived out by Jesus.
> *Respondent in general survey*

---

[105] See, for example, the collection of papers in Scherer and Bevans, *New Directions in Mission and Evangelization* (Orbis, Maryknoll, 1999) vol. III.

challenged and resisted and which have little impact upon the kingdom.

We would draw particular attention to the principles that the Church should express herself in terms accessible to the thought forms and meaning structures of human cultures. There is a need to find dynamic equivalents with which to articulate the truths of faith and a presumption that the Gospel is capable of being proclaimed to all human cultures. Further, there is an expectation of discovering the grace of God already active in the world and in people's lives: the Church should hope to discover 'seeds of the Word' which enable her to 'baptise the culture' without diluting her inheritance of faith through syncretism. Both of the above necessitate dialogue and encounter with the prevailing culture. Also the commitment to one of the above leads to the other.

In encountering the modern world, the Church's social teaching is a necessary component of evangelisation as we meet people in their social, political and economic contexts. In particular this must be a priority in lay formation.[106] The 'preferential option for the poor' and walking with the poor in mission have a particular priority.

We would observe three strands, the religious, the cultural and the socio-economic.

Religious context

We have already alluded to evangelisation taking place in a situation between Christendom and paganism. Much recent discussion of 'New Evangelisation' recognises this. The *General Directory for Catechesis* (1997) notes three distinct situations for evangelisation and catechesis:

- The situation where Christ is not known.
- The situation with strong existing Christian communities.
- An intermediate situation where there have been strong Christian communities, but many baptised are not

[106] *Christifideles Laici* 60.

practising and Christian points of reference are present but often incomplete, fragmentary or exterior to people's lives.[107]

England and Wales today show all of these situations, although perhaps the last is the one that most demands our attention. The Gospel is not alien to England and Wales: our nations have long been evangelised. This evangelisation has affected much of our culture, our laws and our history, and its influence remains far-reaching. Many attitudes within Western culture, and in particular within England and Wales, can be traced to our Christian inheritance. There is a Christian sympathy within our culture which means that we are able to easily find resonances with the Gospel and have points of contact with those who live in an implicitly Christian way without explicit Christian belief, practice or institutional adherence. Yet there is a feeling that within this predominantly Christian background, contemporary Christian practice is a minority option. Within this mix we can see that many of those who have had some sacramental initiation do not practise; some who have had no Christian initiation strongly promote values consonant with the Gospel.

In our nations there may be more than two-thirds of people who believe in God, are conscious of sin and will pray, yet belonging to religious institutions has declined.[108] Indeed some would claim that the UK population, in terms of adherence to organised religion, is one of the least religious in the world.[109] Although some of our efforts at evangelisation must be to convince people to believe, this suggests that the more pressing work is to persuade people to belong. The edges of the Church are often fuzzy.

There is a significant social trend between age cohorts. 66 percent of the 18-24 age band have no religious adherence,

[107] Cf. *General Directory for Catechesis* 58.

[108] See Grace Davie, *Religion in Britain since 1945: believing without belonging* (1994), p. 78, for some collated statistics on these points.

[109] See Nick Dirk De Graaf and Ariana Need in Roger Jowell *et al.*, *British Social Attitudes* (Sage, Aldershot, 2000), ch. 6, for a discussion of this and further statistics.

whereas only 24 percent of those over 65 do not belong to any religion. This correlates with division on attitudes to moral questions and political involvement. There is some debate as to whether this is *life-cycle* or *generational,* that is to say, whether people choose to consider religious questions and adopt religious practices as they get older or whether those in the older cohort who show more commitment to religion showed the same commitment when younger. At one level one would expect life-cycle developments in religious practice and certainly mature adult faith is distinct from childhood faith. However, recent research suggests that trends are largely generational.[110] Given this likelihood, there is a special need for the Gospel to be proclaimed and enacted among younger people, perhaps especially younger adults, and the under-represented generations in Church life. The ethos of schools and colleges, the witness of Christian young people and Christians working alongside young people, the role of chaplaincy in schools and universities and the provision of appropriate retreats, festivals, pilgrimages and other opportunities for young people to encounter the Gospel and the Church must be considered vital.

Within the religious context we must also recognise that many within our nations are committed adherents of world faiths other than Christianity. There is a tension between dialogue and proclamation: we are caught between the temptations of absolute relativism and proselytism. Our primary attitude to men and women of good will must be one of respect. Those who have in their lives 'some ray of the divine light'[111] should be our companions on the road to God.

We must take seriously the Christian life of our ecumenical partners. Our attitude must be one of co-operation rather than competition. This is both because they are our partners in mission and because we are all affected by similar social forces as we all seek to bring the Good News of Jesus to our common neighbours. This commonality of neighbours is particularly the

---

[110] See Alison Park in Jowell *et al., British Social Attitudes*, ch. 1, for a fuller discussion of this position and detailed statistics.

[111] Vatican II, *Nostra Aetate* 2.

case now that the substantial increase in the Catholic population through immigration seems to have levelled off.[112] Further, we are aware that many who make an adult decision to become Catholics have often had involvement (to varying degrees) with other Christian traditions. For many their first proclamation of and response to the Gospel was outside the Catholic Church, even if they subsequently found a home within Catholicism.[113]

Although statistics in this field are notoriously unreliable and difficult to interpret, it has been suggested that the Catholic Church in England and Wales, after some years of maintaining relatively impressive numbers of Mass attenders is now undergoing significant decline. At the same time, other Christian bodies, who had previously suffered decline, seem to be stabilising in terms of numbers. A few groups, New Churches and Pentecostal Churches (definitions of these groups often overlap), have seen significant growth.[114]

We must also consider part of the context of Catholicism in England and Wales itself. Whereas previous generations of Catholics in our nations perceived themselves as within a fortress, often a refuge for immigrants, in which a distinct Catholic subculture could develop, it is now clear that Catholics are much more integrated into the general social trends of England and Wales. The decline of the fortress mentality has both allowed greater dialogue and involvement with our neighbours in civil society and public life but also removed some of the forces which held together the Catholic community.[115] Certainly some of our respondents seemed to

[112] See M. Hornsby-Smith, *Roman Catholics in England* (CUP, Cambridge 1987), pp. 116-132, and Mary J. Hickman in Hornsby-Smith (ed.), *Catholics in England 1950-2000* (Cassell, London 1999), pp. 182-198.

[113] Hornsby-Smith, *Roman Catholic Beliefs in England* (CUP, Cambridge 1991), p. 4, cites 'nearly one in nine' of English Catholics as being converts, primarily from other Christian traditions.

[114] See Peter Brierley (ed.), *UK Christian Handbook Religious Trends 2000/2001* (Christian Research and Harper Collins, London 1999), for a comparative collection of statistics - although the measurements do not always compare like with like and frequently include estimates.

[115] See Hornsby-Smith (1999), pp. 3-24, and the paper in the same book by Sheridan Gilley, pp. 29-45.

wish for a retrenchment into old certainties, an option that other respondents would clearly feel as repressive.

A final part of our religious context to be considered is the decline in vocations to the priesthood and religious life. Although this has been a positive development in pushing the welcome growth of lay ministries and collaborative ministries, nonetheless the decline in numbers of candidates for priestly ordination has had more negative consequences, not least in profoundly skewing the age profile of clergy, forcing fewer priests to maintain punishing work schedules whilst being spread more thinly and suffering increasing stress and its consequences. Allied to this is the question of morale and stress among clergy and parishes engendered by the necessary processes of reorganisation and the introduction of substantial new pastoral plans in many dioceses. From the perceived danger of being an over-clericalised Church, the Catholic Church in England and Wales may find itself in the position of promoting a eucharistic ecclesiology without sufficient priests to celebrate the Eucharist. This eucharistic famine is a long way off in this country but it is necessary to address it now.[116] Although all Christians have a right and duty to engage in evangelisation, there is no doubt that clergy and religious have valuable and essential roles in Catholic evangelisation.

Cultural contexts

While it is sometimes tempting to talk of 'Anglo-Saxon' culture and to point towards features of the dominant historic cultural forces in our nations, it is very difficult to see how this expresses itself today. Not least as the Catholic Church in England and Wales we must recognise that the Welsh experience of whatever might be understood by 'Anglo-Saxon' culture is very different

[116] In comparison to many Catholic Bishops' Conference regions, England and Wales has a healthy ratio of priests to people. The global figure suggests one priest to approximately 2,500 Catholics whereas England and Wales are blessed with a ratio of one priest to every 750 Catholics. Cf. {www.catholic-ew.org.uk/stats}.

from what might be perceived in England. Moreover, the cultural forces in our nations have long been a mosaic. Indeed our Catholic communities contain within themselves an extraordinary cultural mix. It is our contention that there is today little unitary culture in England and Wales but rather each person relates to a series of cultural forms. Some ethnic groups hold a cultural commitment to religious practice and belief yet these traditional ties of culture and religion often seem to be loosening.[117] Within the religious context of diversity referred to above we must also recognise the reality of racism and ethnic and religious discrimination. Part of the Good News is that all people are precious to God, every man and woman is made in the image of God and that all are called into the fullness of God's *eschata*. These must lead us to be very sensitive to racism and to do all within our power to resist it. This both includes our attitudes to our neighbours who may not be Christians and the way we as a Church act internally. We are a multiracial and multiethnic Church in which every member must be honoured. Indeed English Catholic history has had very substantial experience of being a Church with a high proportion of immigrants and of being discriminated against on grounds of religion and/or ethnicity.[118]

There are a number of strong cultural forces present in our nations but there also seems to be a high degree of fragmentation. Youth cultures represent an example of this fragmentation - as well as a series of influences with which some in the Church seek to engage. We should be careful of forcing young people into compartments - you are under

[117] See Mary J. Huckman, 'The Religio-Ethnic Identities of Teenagers of Irish Descent' in Hornsby-Smith (1999), pp. 182-198, for both the maintenance of a 'collective-expressive' cultural and religious identity and its possible lessening by convergence with English models of Catholicism or secularisation. The Irish contribution to Catholicism in England and Wales must be recognised as of particular significance.

[118] Hornsby-Smith (1991), p. 4, cites one quarter of English Catholics as being first generation immigrants and a fifth as being second generation immigrants. See also Myrna Lubin *et al.*, *Black Catholics Speak* (CARJ, London, 1991), for stories of cultural diversity within the English Catholic community.

twenty-one therefore you like dance music and vegetarian food. The diversity of personality types, tastes, and the mystery of being human are as rich among contemporary young people as they are amongst any other generation. Many choices exist today and many different choices are made: there is therefore not a single youth culture. That being said we should note some trends. There is a post-secular trend: spirituality, mystery, non-empirical and aesthetic desires and even ritual are often seen as positive things. Some young people value community and a strong framework within which to live. But one frequently meets significant distrust of authorities and institutions: this is often expressed in terms of individualism and a sense of the right to make personal choices. This leads to a high degree of moral relativism and an emphasis on personal pleasure. There is also a high degree of moral indignation, not least about environmental issues and the destructive potential of global capitalism. Some young people display powerful and passionate commitments, even while many of their peers seem to be apathetic and without any focus. Many young people are happily exploring the possibilities of new technologies; others show a technophobic suspicion. Some of these trends may appear paradoxical but their very variety underlines the point that many options are open to youth cultures which are likely to become ever more pluralistic and amorphous. Both 'yob culture' and the World Youth Day in Rome in the Holy Year 2000 are actual, if contradictory, contemporary expressions of youth cultures.

We have also witnessed major changes in marriage and family life. Patterns of unmarried co-habitation, children born outside marriage, marriage breakdown, children brought up with one parent, remarriage after divorce and children brought up with step-parents are common and co-exist alongside more traditional and, for the Church more comfortable, patterns of marriages and families.[119] Likewise there is increasing social

---

[119] See Timothy Buckley CSsR, *What Binds Marriage? Roman Catholic Theology in Practice* (Geoffrey Chapman, London, 1997) and his article 'English Catholics and Divorce' in Hornsby-Smith (1999).

acceptance of a range of lifestyles, sexualities and non-traditional forms of families including same sex relationships. People today experience a wide range of role models as to how to form relationships and how to raise children. This social reality is within the Catholic community as well as a trend in the general population.

A particular and important cultural trend is to emphasise the value of women. Contemporary society has made substantial gains in promoting gender equality and enabling women to play a full economic, political and social role. While many would say that society still has more work to do in this

> I feel very strongly that the Catholic Church lags behind the wider community in sexual equality. We should be prosecuted!
> *Respondent to general survey*

field, more would suggest that the Catholic Church here offers less 'Good News' than secular culture. The Catholic Church as an institution is often perceived as both anti-feminist and anti-women. Although one may point to strong statements upon the dignity and value of women and initiatives to include women in deliberative and consultative bodies as well as a host of individual Catholics committed to a just empowerment of women, there is a sense that women are not treated as equal to men and are frequently excluded from key aspects of Church life. Such perception mitigates against the evangelising mission of the Church. Not least, it has been frequently cited as a reason why those who have been part of the Catholic community have chosen to leave the Church.

Several of these issues concern late modernity and post-modernity. Although there is much debate about the precise meanings of these terms, from our perspective they express themselves in such things as individualism, materialism, economism and secularism (late Modernity) and the end of the great stories,[120] the demise of overarching authorities and

---

[120] *Le fin des grands récits* is associated with Jean Francois Lyotard: the collapse of metanarratives - such as Marxism - is seen as one of the core characteristics of Post-Modernism.

ideologies, eclecticism, playful combinations of ideas and themes and impermanence (Post-Modernism).

All these realities challenge the Church both to witness to the traditions she has received and to minister to and evangelise contemporary culture in England and Wales. More fundamentally they ask the question, 'what is good news in modern culture?' In these circumstances the Church must become transparently and obviously good news; such renewal is necessary in its own right but is also the essential condition of sharing good news.

Socio-economic context

Any evangelisation which ignores the need to accompany the poorest and most needy in society is incomplete and fails to demonstrate one of the hallmarks of the kingdom of God and our Lord's own declaration of the Gospel.[121] As Pope John Paul II has emphasised there is a 'special presence of Christ in the poor, and this requires the Church to make a preferential option for them'.[122]

> 'We must ... ensure that in every Christian community the poor feel at home. Would not this approach be the greatest and most effective presentation of the good news of the Kingdom?'[123]

The socio-economic context of England and Wales contains many challenges for the Church, including internal divisions and global responsibilities. The Gospel of justice requires the Church to engage with these issues. Indeed the promotion of 'Justice, Peace and the Integrity of Creation', much in vogue in international missiological convergence is a Gospel imperative for the Catholic Church in England and Wales. The experience of overseas mission may have been the engine for promoting

---

[121] Cf. Luke 4:16f. and Matthew 25:31-46.
[122] *Novo Millennio Ineunte* 49.
[123] *Novo Millennio Ineunte* 50.

serious and radical Gospel questioning of social, economic and political structures, but the need to do so also applies to our local situation. The Jubilee call of the Holy Year called for a righting of all imbalances in society. This examination of how we relate to each other, to the land and to God brought into focus our constant vocation to resist the *mysterium iniquitas* with the hope, vision and reality of Divine love - that there may be peace with justice and justice with forgiveness.[124]

The phrase 'Civil Society' has had something of a vogue recently. At one level this refers to that sphere of activity between the private and the state. In this area, the Church as an institution, together with other voluntary associations, is a significant contributor. However, 'Civil Society' also has at least two more controversial political meanings. The one is a vision of a peaceable well ordered society in which people are well behaved towards one another: while this is a laudable thing the Church may be co-opted as an agent of social control in achieving this. The second, and related to this, is the notion promoted by President George W. Bush, and given some support by British politicians, for faith-based organisations being given a lead role in providing care and welfare services.

The existence of the socially excluded and areas of significant deprivation in both urban and rural areas is a cause of concern for the Church's mission. The document *The Common Good and the Catholic Church's Social Teaching* (1996) raised both some controversy and several important points. It showed a commitment by the local Church in the corporate person of the Bishops' Conference to engage with the social and political situation of England and Wales in the light of Catholic social teaching. As such it was both a vehicle for dissemination of Catholic social teaching to the people of God in these nations, a reflection of the implications of this in our context and an attempt to address decision makers in national and local government.

Focussed single issue campaigns have often been occasions when people have felt a powerful synthesis between faith and

[124] See Pope John Paul II, Message for World Peace Day 2002.

life. Certainly examples which demonstrate this include Pax Christi[125] and the Campaign Against the Arms Trade,[126] pro-life initiatives[127] and the Jubilee 2000 (Jubilee Plus)[128] campaign to cancel the debt burden on developing and under-developed nations.

Broad Based Organising has been a particular instance when Christians in company and alliance with others have been involved in active promotion of the common good in their neighbourhoods.

There is also the lobbying of Government and decision makers. One way in which the bishops have expressed their role as evangelisers has been their work of advocacy with national and local government politicians and officers.

In the face of globalisation, the UK represents those with economic, political and military power over others, and this demands particular responsibilities in many fields including business ethics, environmental sustainability and threat of ecological damage as well as the economic development of poorer and often dependent nations and peoples.

One location where poverty in England and Wales meets with the effects of globalisation is the continuing tension over asylum seekers.

[125] See {www.paxchristi.net} and {www.paxchristi.org.uk}.

[126] See {www.caat.org.uk}.

[127] There are several groups active in this field but examples may be found at {www.lifeuk.org} and {www.spuc.org.uk}.

[128] See {www.jubilee2000uk.org}.

5. Frameworks of analysis

We have found two frameworks helpful in identifying aspects of evangelisation: both of them were consciously in our mind in preparing our survey questionnaire and in observing practitioners of evangelisation and consulting with our lens groups.

The first we have already commented upon in discussing the nature of evangelisation and mission.

a) The triangle of New Testament concepts represented by *kerygma*, *koinonia* and *diakonia*.[129]

Kerygma: the apostolic proclamation - announcing the good news to those who have not heard it with the explicit intention of forming new Christians and furthering the kingdom of God. This outreach is fundamental to the identity of the Church and is the purpose of the Church.

Koinonia: the participation and sharing of life which is rooted in the mutuality and union of the Divine Persons in the Trinity, is mediated to the Church, especially in the sacraments, and is expressed in the fellowship of believers. Such communion (*communio*) is both the pattern of the Church in the world and the gift of the Church to the world.

Diakonia: the life of service is a necessary component of the Good News. This service is necessary for both the above aspects of evangelisation. It also has an essential expression in the service of the 'poor of the Lord' (*anawim YHWH*). Love of neighbour, especially our neighbours in need of whatever kind, is expected of the Church in mission.

b) The process of Christian formation as experienced through the catechumenate and presented in the *General Directory of Catechesis* and elsewhere. We would wish to stress the importance and centrality of the *Rite of Christian Initiation of*

---

[129] See Bosch, *Transforming Mission*, p. 511f. Adrian Hastings, 'The diversities of Mission', *Missionalia* 24 (1) 1996, pp. 3-16. See also Madge Karechi, 'A Missing Link: A Response to Adrian Hastings' irreducible triangle of the Church', *Missionalia* 25 (1) 1997, pp. 124-134.

Adults and related processes to the Church's understanding and methodology of evangelisation.

- Pre-evangelisation: Christian presence in the world and witness to the world.
- Initial evangelisation: the explicit presentation of Christ and openness to enquiry from those on the margins of the Church.
- Catechumenate: the deepening personal encounter with Christ and his Church - exploring faith and the synthesis of faith and life.
- Enlightenment: the sacramental preparation for initiation.
- *Mystagogia*: the ongoing growth in the mysteries of God, Christ, the Church and the kingdom - development of personal vocation and ministry in and for the people of God.

These steps in the Christian journey are not hermetically sealed compartments. Indeed one of the features of 'New Evangelisation' is that we should expect partial or incomplete experience of several of these stages - for example, we may encounter people who have been sacramentally initiated yet who have not had a deep personal encounter with Christ and his Church, or we may find people whose witness to Gospel values is profound yet have no explicit commitment to the Church.

Some of those we talked to suggested that the contemporary Catholic Church was good at the second and third steps of this journey (catechumenate and sacramental preparation) and had some, if patchy, strength in the last part but was weak at the direct kerygmatic proclamation of the Gospel to those who were outside the Church. That is to say, where people had come to a decision to ask for sacramental initiation, the Catholic Church has healthy and developing structures and processes and a good network of catechists but there is a less developed series of activities which encourage people to come to that point of decision. However, there were divergent opinions about this and indeed we were able to discuss these matters with several groups for whom direct initial kerygmatic proclamation was their primary intention. Much activity of groups concerned with evangelisation was in effect a contribution to *mystagogia* - addressing those who had already been initiated so that they may further grow in the mystery of faith and develop ministries which would contribute to the mission of the Church in their local situations. (Hence, for instance, the CMS mission process with its stress on developing faith sharing, scriptural reflection, collaborative ministry and group work.)

Parish vitality

A few people objected in particular to the way our survey included questions to measure parish vitality. We investigated the vitality of parish communities for several reasons:

1. We had a Catholic presupposition that the life of those gathered around the altar should be a beacon shining out into the world and drawing people into the life of God in Christ celebrated by that community. That the Church should be a sacrament of communion for the world seems to us to be a key insight since the Second Vatican Council.[130] The Triune God comes to his people through the sending of the Son and the Holy Spirit: the divine communion of love, through love, reaches out. The Church is formed by this outreach of God (*Missio Dei*) and is both a witness to the divine communion and an agent of the continuing divine movement to draw all into communion.[131] The goal of mission is this life of love, which we may represent as the kingdom of God, not simply the Church.[132]

---

[130] See Extraordinary Synod of Bishops, 1985, On the Implementation of the Second Vatican Council. *L'Osservatore Romano (Weekly English Edition)*, 16 December 1985, and *Novo Millennio Ineunte* 42-50.

[131] Cf. *Ad Gentes* 2.

[132] Cf. *Redemptoris Missio* 12-15 esp 15. 'The kingdom aims at transforming human relationships; it grows gradually as people slowly learn to love, forgive and serve one another. Jesus sums up the whole Law, focusing it on the commandment of love. ... The kingdom's nature, therefore, is one of communion among all human beings - with one another and with God. The kingdom is the concern of everyone: individuals, society, and the world. Working for the kingdom means

2. We also had a further Catholic assumption that the visible society of the Church should be intimately connected with the mystical body. A personal relationship with Christ includes incorporation into the Body of Christ. Being a Christian is therefore not simply individual acceptance of an argument over the nature and work of Christ but sharing in the grace-filled and incarnated community which Christ forms. The People of God are not to be placed into an idealised compartment, but the actual human quality of life we share together and with others is a participation in the things of God. The Gospel is best expressed in its being lived out by the grace-filled community and in its members - before the doctrinal reflection of that life. For many therefore *belonging* has a priority over *believing*.[133] A desire to be part of this community, and being attracted to the community precedes accepting what the community believes. This coheres with the insight that faith is caught more than taught: a vital parish becomes a place where people experience faith and instils in them a desire to be part of a community of faith.

3. Pragmatically we considered that the vitality of a community was important in enabling the community to be a place of witness, a place of welcome, a place of catechesis and a

---

acknowledging and promoting God's activity, which is present in human history and transforms it. Building the kingdom means working for liberation from evil in all its forms. In a word, the kingdom of God is the manifestation and the realization of God's plan of salvation in all its fullness.'

[133] We are conscious that for many Catholics their religious identity is described in terms of the community they are committed to rather than to a check list of doctrines and even less to a series of moral propositions. See Hornsby-Smith (1987), pp. 47-66. However, it is also our feeling that the emphasis in evangelisation today must be about building relationships in community as suggested by the rich theological implications of communion. Cf. Robin Gill in *Vision for Growth* (SPCK, London, 1994), p. 27f. This does not cut across the observation in our post-Christendom, not entirely Pagan society, that there are significant numbers of people who believe without belonging. Cf. Grace Davie, *Religion in Britain since 1945: believing without belonging* (Blackwell, Oxford, 1994).

place of growth in faith and discipleship. There are several elements that can be used to measure this vitality. This acknowledges the insights of some evangelical initiatives (such as the Church Growth Movement and the related Natural Church Development[134]) as well as the results of the international and ecumenical Church Life Survey[135] and the ecumenical British project 'Building Bridges of Hope'.[136]

4. The question had also been raised that Catholic parishes themselves, partly because of some feeling of a lack of parish vitality, were not the foci of evangelisation but rather other ecclesial realities had become more significant. Small groups, communities, movements, conferences etc. may be the leading edge of the contemporary Church and the place where people discovered the excitement and energy of the Gospel and where they could experience personal, ecclesial and social transformation. Many parishioners, parish priests and particularly seminarians claimed significant contacts with such groups but the parish remains the central focus of evangelisation.

[134] 'Natural Church Development' recognises eight factors which researchers found in what they perceived to be growing Churches: empowering leadership, gift-oriented ministry, passionate spirituality, functional structures, inspiring worship, holistic small groups, need-oriented evangelism and loving relationships. While Catholic expectations of such factors will differ from this list there is a clear correlation here between Church vitality and Church growth. More details on this may be found in Christian A. Schwartz, *Natural Church Development: a practical guide to a new approach,* and at {www.bcga.org.uk}.

[135] {www.ncls.org.au}. Although the Catholic Church in Australia is taking part in this survey, the Catholic Church in England and Wales is not participating in the UK element.

[136] *Building Bridges of Hope* is an ecumenical project which includes Catholic participants. It has discovered seven key learnings about churches which build effective bridges for mission in their local community are those which are: focusing vision, building local partnerships, sharing faith and values, nourishing daily living, developing shared leadership, becoming communities of learning and being accompanied. For more details see the Video and Study Guide *Bridges to Build* (CCOM) and at {www.ctbi.org.uk/bbh}.

6. Statistical analyses of questionnaire data

The information contained in this chapter is largely based on data gathered from the largest of the surveys conducted during the research, namely that addressed to parishioners. In the main the overall pattern of responses to each of the other surveys conducted is not proportionally different in any marked degree from that which is illustrated here. However, where there are notable differences in response between the different constituencies surveyed then these have been indicated.

Many of the questions for which responses are outlined in this chapter requested participants to indicate more than one choice from a list of several options as opposed to indicating a single response. Where this is the case the percentages shown in the charts add up to more than 100 percent.

The information below is set out according to a series of categories for ease of illustration.

Parish vitality

The first series of questions addressed to the participants of each survey was aimed at gauging parish vitality in order to develop some sort of picture of the health of the corporate life of the local church. The assumption at work here is that it is still largely the parish that people look to as a sign of the Church in action at the local level. Equally, the parish is viewed as constituting the 'home' of those who belong to the community of faith: whether fully integrated within it, on the fringes, having left the 'household' or amongst those who are in the process of coming to faith for the first time.

In part, therefore, the intention of such questioning was to try to discern the extent to which the local church is itself 'Good News' in accordance with the view that:

'At its best, a parish is a community of baptised, committed believers, who, empowered by the Holy Spirit, give witness to Christ among themselves and in the world.'[137]

Hence, underlying the questions regarding parish vitality is the assumption that evangelisation works best in the context of a church that is itself good news.

Figure 1 reflects an age and gender profile amongst those who might be described as 'active' within the general parish population which is not uncommon in terms of Church membership nationally and which is broadly in tune with findings from other recent surveys, most notably the Church Life Profile 2001. Namely, that the overwhelming majority of those actively involved in the life of the local Church are over 36 years of age and predominantly female.

Overall there is a male:female ratio of 2:3 with men making up 39% (of those who disclosed their gender) and women 61%. There are more women than men in every age group. This imbalance is most prominent between the ages of 26 and 50 whilst there is a much lower predominance of women amongst those under 25.

These findings indicate an ageing and declining Church population and point to a situation in the future whereby, based on present demographics trends in Church involvement, there is likely to be an accelerated decrease in the number of Mass attending parishioners. It is well reported that Catholic marriages and infant baptisms have fallen dramatically in recent decades. For instance, in the five-year period between 1994 and 1999 it is estimated that Catholic baptisms in England and Wales declined by 16% and marriages by 30%.[138] By implication it would appear that the Church is not very effective in attracting or retaining young adults.

---

[137] Clare Barbour, *Priests and People*, vol. 15, nn. 8 & 9, August/September 2001, pp. 311-315.

[138] Percentages are based on statistics presented in the *Catholic Directory 2001* and *1995*. Published on behalf of the Bishops' Conference of England and Wales by Gabriel Communications Ltd.

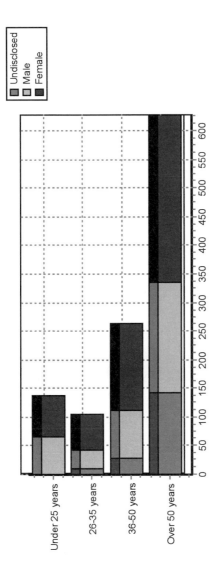

Figure 1: Age/Gender of respondents to General Survey

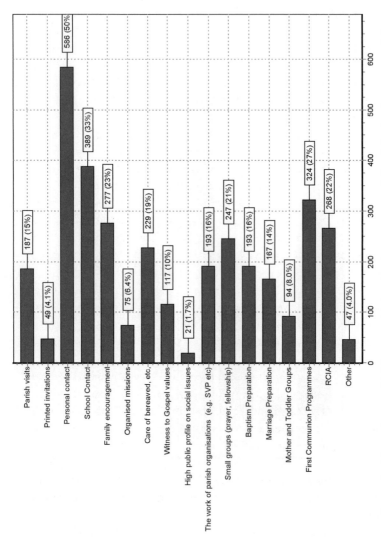

Figure 2: Where do you think your parish has been most successful at bringing in new people?

There may, however, be a faint glimmer of hope in this respect represented in the findings from the survey by the slightly higher response rate, in particular from males, amongst those in the under 25 age group when compared to those aged 26-35. This may, however, be an over optimistic representation of the real picture. Whatever accounts for this contrast, young people (i.e. those under 36) still account for less than 20% of the active local Church community. There are very clearly serious long-term implications for evangelisation in relation to children, young people and the formation of Catholic families if the Church is to remain vital.

In response to the question illustrated in figure 2 - Where do you think your parish has been most successful at bringing in new people? - participants were at liberty to indicate up to three choices. Amongst all those surveyed, personal contact was seen to be by far the most important factor in encouraging new people to join the parish community. Half of all parishioners, 67% of parish priests and 63% of diocesan officers and other professionals saw personal contact as the single most important factor in bringing new people into the Church.

One interesting aspect of these responses is that across the range of surveys conducted, school contact is consistently seen to be the second most influential factor (33%) in bringing new people into a parish. One might have anticipated that more influence than is evidenced from the results would be attributed to the impact of sacramental programmes as opportunities for evangelisation, particularly in relation to children and families.

Of the sacramental programmes listed, preparation for first communion is considered the most effective (27%) in attracting new people to the parish community. Considerably less influence is attributed to the impact of preparation for baptism (16%) and marriage (14%). Other factors influential in attracting newcomers include family encouragement, RCIA and small groups.

It is perhaps interesting to reflect that when asked where their parish has been most successful in attracting newcomers only 10% of respondents cited 'witness to Gospel values' as a factor.

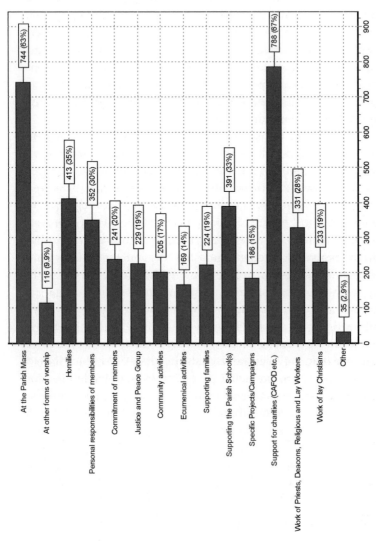

Figure 3: Where do you think that your parish most engages with the needs of the world?

There are very clearly two particular spheres in which participants feel that their parish most engages with the needs of the world (figure 3). Namely, support for charities such as CAFOD (67%), and in the context of the parish Mass (63%). Roughly one third of respondents consider homilies, parish schools and personal responsibilities to be areas in which their parish is actively engaged with the world's needs. Justice and Peace, the work of lay Christians, supporting families (each 19%), community activities (17%) and ecumenical activities (14%) are indicated as areas where the parish is generally least engaged with the needs of the world.

In relation to parish vitality the intention was in part to discover from participants how satisfied they were with provision in their parish for certain groups of people.

On the whole the respondents appear to be largely happy with what is offered in their parish for children and the elderly (figure 4). 56% of parishioners being 'very' or 'extremely' satisfied with the provision for children. The same cannot be said in response to young adults and single people where only 17% and 11% respectively could be described as generally happy with what is offered for these groups. This situation raises clear concerns in the light of the demographic structure outlined in figure 1 since the groups apparently being least well served in the parish community are precisely those that it would seem most crucial to retain for the future health of the Church. Most obvious from the data is the lack of satisfaction in terms of the support and encouragement of single people in parishes.

Option	No reply %	Not at all %	Not much %	Modera-tely so %	Very much %	Extre-mely so %
Children	4.4	3.7	9.3	25	34	22
Young adults	7.8	15	32	26	11	5.7
Single	12	17	32	26	7.4	3.2
Married couples	11	10	18	35	17	6.2
Family	7.3	5.9	11	30	30	14
Elderly	5.4	5.4	11	29	32	15

Figure 4a: How satisfied are you with what is offered
in your parish for these groups?

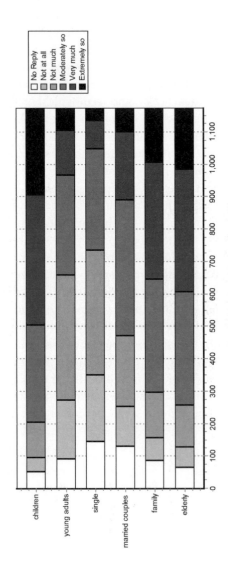

Figure 4b: How satisfied are you with what is offered in your parish for these groups?

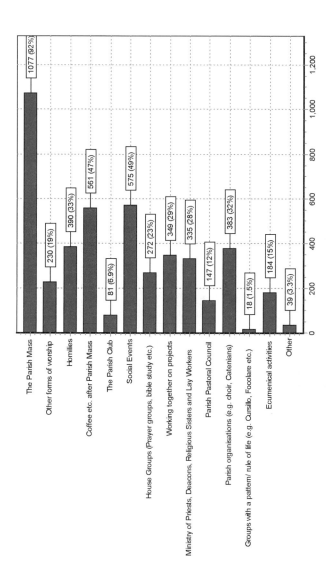

Figure 5: What do you think most builds Christian fellowship in your parish?

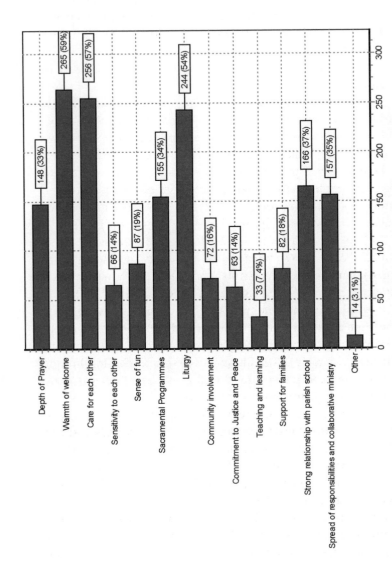

Figure 6: What would say are the greatest strengths of your parish?

According to the remit of the research it also appeared appropriate to try and gauge the extent to which the Church in the local context is a place where its members can experience true Christian fellowship as part of the Body of Christ. Hence, participants were asked to reflect on the sorts of parish activities that best enabled the development of true community within their parish. The results of such a question are illustrated in figure 5.

The most outstanding contribution in this regard (92%) is attributed to the parish Mass. In addition almost half of those surveyed (49%) suggest that social events and gatherings after Mass (47%) are important aspects of building fellowship.

Homilies and parish organisations such as the choir and Catenians are important amongst one third of respondents. The influence of working on parish projects and the ministry of priests and other parish professionals is slightly less influential.

23% of respondents highlighted the contribution of 'house groups' (i.e. for prayer, bible study etc.) which is markedly more than the number of participants who mentioned groups with a pattern or rule of life such as Cursillo and Focolare (1.5%).

It is interesting to note that there is a strong correspondence in relation to the most important factors in building community as with those that help participants most in integrating life and faith (see figure 11). Namely, that worship (including liturgy, sermons and the parish Mass) and social events consistently produce the top answers in each instance.

In general the main strengths of the parish (figure 6) are seen to be its warmth of welcome and degree of care for members, in addition to the liturgy - each of these factors being highlighted by over half the respondents. 37% of parish priests saw strengths in the relationship with the parish school and to a slightly lesser extent collaborative ministry.

One third of priests viewed sacramental programmes and depth of prayer as particular strengths. Markedly lower responses were attributed to community involvement, commitment to Justice and Peace, and even more strikingly to teaching and learning.

The responses to the following question - Where is the Gospel most proclaimed and/or enacted in your parish? (figure 7) - are revealing in relation to the locations in which participants believe witness to the Gospel to be demonstrated in the local church. For instance, it is very evident that the overwhelming majority of respondents consider that the Gospel is most proclaimed and enacted in the internal parish setting of the Mass (93%) and to a significantly lesser extent in the work of ordained, religious and lay parish professionals (50%) and parish schools (43%).

What is striking in comparison is that less than one quarter of respondents appear to see the family as an important location in which the Gospel is directly lived out and less than half as many again (9.3%) indicate that there is a significant contribution on behalf of the parish in proclaiming the Gospel in the broader community

Even more apparent is that under 2% of participants consider the work environment to be a place in which either proclamation or witness to the Gospel is apparent. Indeed, the workplace seems to be the location in which the Gospel is perceived to be the least proclaimed and enacted of all the given options.

However, some caution is required in addressing this question. For instance, it is possible that the extremely low percentage response for the 'workplace' (1.7%) indicates that participants interpreted this to refer to the structure and culture of the work environment in terms of institutional systems as opposed to the more personal relationships and interactions which might be perceived to be inferred within the option 'lives/work of lay Christians' and which receives a considerably higher response (33%). However, one of our ecumenical consultants points out that:

> this finding is corroborated by the work done some years ago by Christians in Public Life and indeed in *Building Bridges of Hope*. There is widespread evidence that church is not felt good at supporting Christians' witness in the workplace.[139]

[139] The Rev. Donald Elliot in an email.

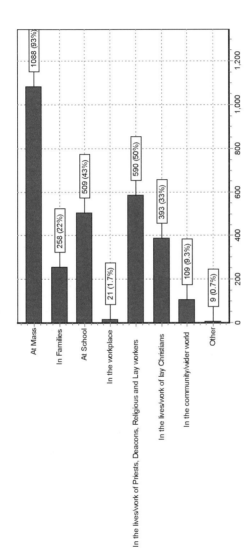

Figure 7: Where is the Gospel most proclaimed and/or enacted in your parish?

Nevertheless, the responses illustrated in figure 7 tend to confirm what is largely evident from other questions related to measures of parish vitality in that there is a marked tendency for the parish to be inward looking with an apparent reluctance to proclaim the Gospel in the broader community or in an overtly secular environment. The picture emerging is one of parishioners, clergy and other diocesan professionals who either feel inadequate to the task of evangelisation beyond the 'safe' surroundings of the parish or who do not perceive such missionary activity as part of the Church's sacred calling.

However, despite the tendency to be insular, the overall responses received across the different constituencies indicate that the parish is the primary location of evangelisation in the local church and neighbourhood. It is here that people searching for God and for meaning in their lives come with their deepest questions, desires and concerns in the hope of company and guidance for their journey amongst the faithful of the parish. Hence, according to the surveys it is still the parish that people primarily look to as a place of witness and welcome.

Perceptions of evangelisation

The most obvious things that come to mind on hearing the word 'evangelisation' for most people are making new Christians (49%, figure 8) and a feeling that they should be doing more (46%) or a feeling of 'hope' (43%). Only slightly subsidiary to such responses is the perception that 'evangelisation' involves the building of communities and transforming the world. Considerably fewer of those questioned viewed evangelisation as 'Protestant campaigns' (14%) or Church activities overseas (20%).

There appears to be amongst those surveyed an overall breadth of vision as to what evangelisation involves, from reaching the un-churched to the building of communities and the transformation of society.

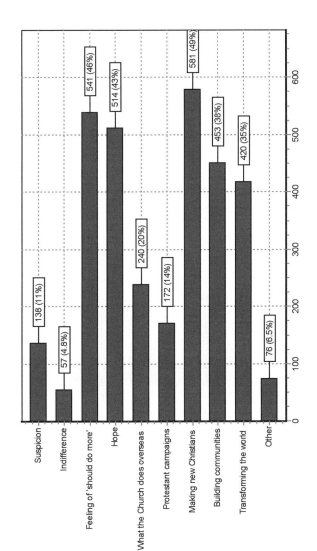

Figure 8: When you hear the word 'evangelisation' what comes into your mind?

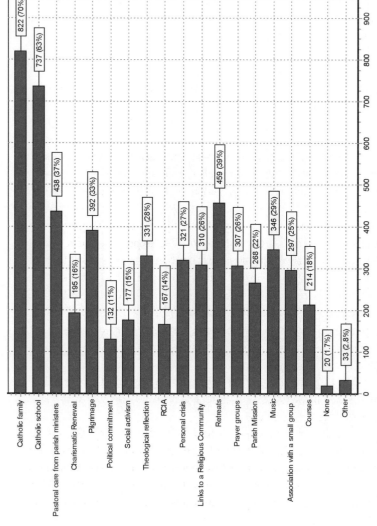

Figure 9: What aspects of the stories most speak to you? (add to perceptions of evangelisation)

I think that evangelisation is much more subtle and demanding than I used to.

Respondent to general survey

The emphasis on hope is echoed in additional comments respondents were encouraged to make in the closing statement of each questionnaire:

I am very hopeful for the future and have a sense of the Holy Spirit renewing the Church. I feel challenged by the present opportunities in the Church.

Respondent to general survey

When asked to comment on specific aspects of four personal faith journeys which they most closely associated with (figure 9) it is very obviously the influence of being nurtured in faith within the context of a Catholic family (70%) and in a Catholic school (63%) that have most effectively brought the gospel 'to life' for the majority of respondents. The experience of retreats, pastoral care and pilgrimages are identified as important factors in evangelisation by roughly one third of the respondents.

Influences related to liturgical music, theological reflection and times of personal crisis are important to a slightly lesser degree and links to a religious community, prayer groups and other small groups are mentioned by a quarter of all participants.

Political commitment, social activism, the RCIA and other courses are important in people's personal evangelisation to a markedly lesser degree.

When asked their view as to whom the Church should be looking to evangelise (figure 10) the categories that headed the list across the two largest constituencies surveyed (parishioners and parish priests) were the 'lapsed' and young families. This response varies only slightly amongst diocesan professionals and seminarians whereby the evangelisation of young families is viewed as being only slightly subsidiary in importance to the evangelisation of young people more generally. Responses relating to the evangelisation of university and secondary

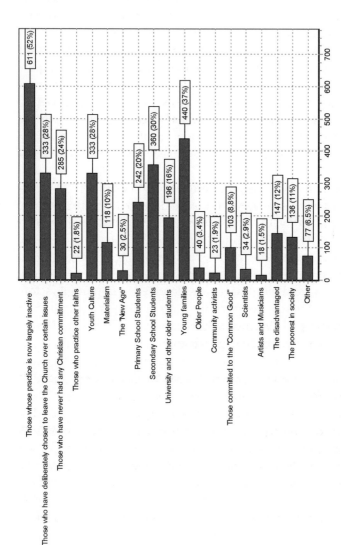

Figure 10: In your opinion, whom should the Church be looking to evangelise?

school students and youth culture receive some of the most high-ranking responses across the different survey groups. Those who have left the Church and those who have no Christian commitment are considered to be notable subsidiary groups in terms of their need for evangelisation.

In terms of the overall picture, the opinion of participants as to whom the Church should be looking to evangelise is quite heavily weighted towards young people and youth culture. Amongst the highest ranking responses 66% more people specified some aspect of youth evangelisation as important compared to the evangelisation of those who could be described as 'inactive' or who have left the Church over particular issues.

Whilst illustrating a breadth of concern for the evangelisation of various groups the data seems to demonstrate very clearly the perception that the evangelisation of young people, in the context of families, universities, schools and the broader youth culture is the sphere in which there is the most pressing need for evangelising activity on behalf of the Church.

Synthesis of life and faith - the Gospel in daily experience

A series of questions was addressed to participants aimed at determining the extent to which they perceived the Gospel to be integrated within various aspects of their daily life. The assumption being that the synthesis of life and faith communicated in the form of 'wordless witness' is an important element of evangelisation in that a life lived in the Gospel will communicate the Gospel to others.

> Evangelisation, for me, is a result of an authentic witness to the Gospel in both words and deeds.
> *Respondent to survey of seminary students*

The two most important factors helping people to synthesise life and faith (figure 11) appear to be the liturgy and

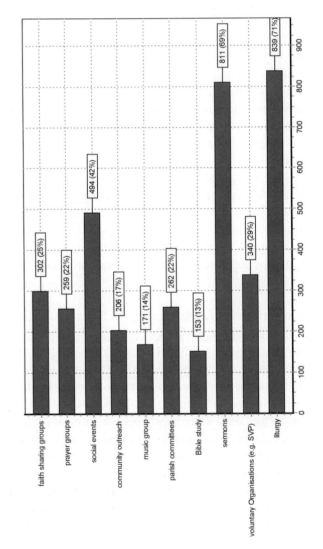

Figure 11: Which aspects of parish life help you the most in relating your faith to everyday life and the wider concerns of society?

sermons (71% and 69% respectively). Less prominent than these but still considered helpful by 42% of respondents are social events.

29% of respondents find engagement in the activities of voluntary organisations such as the SVP helpful in relating faith to everyday life, whilst a quarter of all parishioners find that being part of a faith-sharing group helps them to integrate faith and life. A slightly smaller proportion of those surveyed found prayer groups and parish committees of benefit in this regard. Aspects of parish life considered to be of least influence in relating faith to everyday life include community outreach and Bible study.

The casual observer might regard the high response for preaching with some suspicion. Not least since homilies are not often generally seen to be anticipated as a 'high point' in the experience of common worship. However, there is some evidence to support the validity of these results in the recent findings of the Church Life Profile (April 2001) in which 57% of the 100,000 church attenders surveyed agreed with the statement: 'The preaching I hear in this local church is usually very helpful to me in my everyday life.'

It is evident from the responses that in excess of one third of those surveyed believe that they have a positive impact on the communities in which they live and work (figure 12). Roughly half of all respondents feel that they have a moderate impact and 12% claim to have little or no positive impact in such areas.

When asked about the influence of Gospel values on their actions (figure 13) it is interesting to note that the vast majority of respondents (77%) feel that they are very much guided by Gospel imperatives and only fewer than 4% of those surveyed consider that Gospel values do not really influence their behaviour. Not surprisingly a very similar pattern of responses is apparent when participants are asked about the extent to which the Gospel has influenced their life in general as illustrated in figure 14.

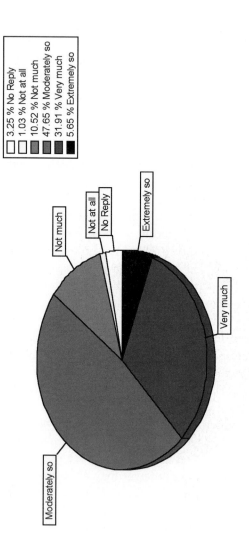

Legend:
- 3.25 % No Reply
- 1.03 % Not at all
- 10.52 % Not much
- 47.65 % Moderately so
- 31.91 % Very much
- 5.65 % Extremely so

Figure 12: To what extent do you think that you have a positive impact on the communities in which you live and work?

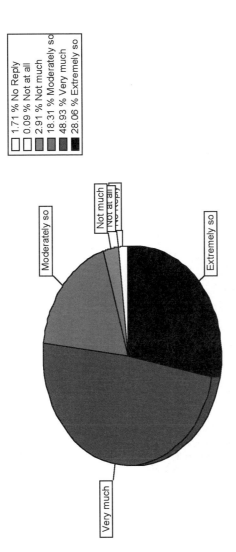

Figure 13: To what extent do you think that Gospel values guide/influence your actions?

1.71 % No Reply
0.09 % Not at all
2.91 % Not much
18.31 % Moderately so
48.93 % Very much
28.06 % Extremely so

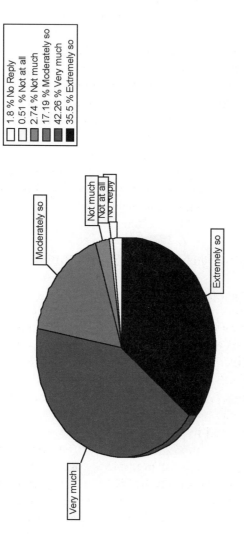

Figure 14: How much would you say that an awareness of the gospel has influenced your life?

It is somewhat striking that despite the fact that 77% of those questioned believe that their personal lives are very much directed by Gospel imperatives, the same people (see figure 12) do not seem to perceive such 'living' as impacting in equal measure, through so called 'wordless witness', on the communities in which they live and work. Such an apparent gap may suggest that participants have the tendency to be less confident and more reticent in bearing witness to the Gospel in more public, or more overtly secular, and less 'safe' surroundings than their usual faith community.

In other words, there may be an equal mismatch between participants' desire to live a life directed according to Gospel values and their actual behaviour in the workplace and the community beyond the parish. For many the desire to 'belong' at work and in the wider community may well in some measure mitigate against authentic witness in these contexts.

RCIA and other sacramental programmes

A variety of questions within the surveys produced responses that relate to the perceived role and importance of RCIA and other sacramental programmes within the parish context.

For instance, it is clear that in many people's perception sacramental programmes perform an important role in bringing new people into a parish. When asked to indicate spheres of parish activity that have an impact in attracting new people, over one third (36%) of the total responses to the question (illustrated in figure 2) indicate one or other type of sacramental programme as being 'most successful' in this respect. Among these, first communion programmes rank most highly followed very closely by RCIA whilst preparation for baptism and marriage are not seen to be quite as influential. Equally the response to further questions gives additional weight to the importance attached in particular to first communion programmes as a gateway for evangelisation. (See figure 20: To what extent have the following ignited a sense of the Gospel?)

One area in which there appears to be a comparatively low response in relation to the influence of RCIA and baptism preparation is in the context of a more directly personal question as to the factors that have 'ignited' a sense of the Gospel in the individual as opposed to previous questions containing sacramental programmes which are addressed more specifically to parish activities. Bearing in mind that the overall age structure of the sample group is predominantly over fifty this is not necessarily a surprising result, since it is perhaps more likely that those in this age group have had no direct personal experience of baptism preparation programmes or RCIA.

When questioned more generally about where most energy is directed in their parish (see figure 22) 45% of participants highlight sacramental programmes as one of the most significant areas of parish activity.

Small groups

The following questions were aimed at elucidating the relative importance of involvement in small groups amongst those who participated in the survey. More particularly, some of the questions were addressed in such a way as to try and ascertain the extent to which involvement in small group activities was effective in terms of fostering a sense of Gospel living.

The highest single response evident when questioned about contact with small groups is from those respondents who have had some connection with CAFOD (figure 15).

One quarter of those questioned indicate some involvement with the CMS, 18% with HCPT, an Alpha course or similar and 12% of those surveyed have had some contact with diocesan youth teams, Taizé, Iona or similar communities.

The groups listed are broad ranging in type but not exhaustive. What is not evident from the responses to this question is the breadth of small groups with which the survey sample claim to have an active involvement. The following paragraphs will expand on this point in a little more detail.

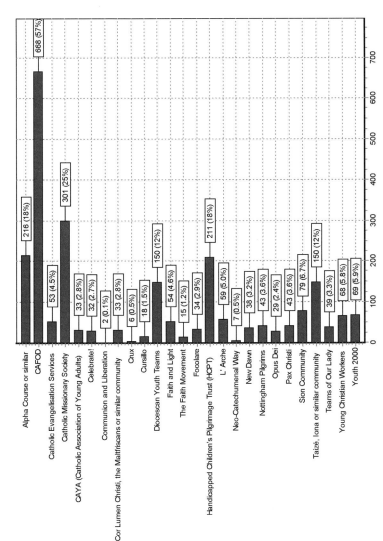

Figure 15: Have you had positive contact with any of these groups or activities?

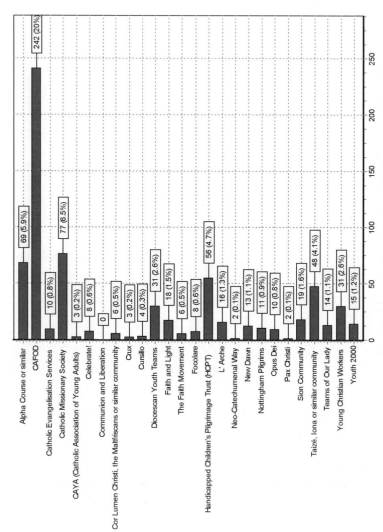

Figure 16: Of the above, which has most fostered in you a sense of the Gospel?

Those who responded to the above question were also asked subsequently to specify which single group out of those they had chosen had most fostered in them a sense of the Gospel. The results to this question are illustrated in figure 16.

20% of respondents indicated CAFOD as the most influential group. Others note the CMS and Alpha (6-7%), HCPT, Taizé and similar communities (4-5%) as having most fostered in them a sense of the Gospel. All other groups listed each account for less than 3% of the views of those questioned.

The list of groups presented to respondents for consideration in this question, was clearly not exhaustive. Hence, in an additional open question participants were asked if they had been influenced more significantly by groups others than those provided in the question and if so to specify the nature of such groups.

In response, 30% of the survey sample indicated that groups other than those listed in figure 16 had influenced them more. The range of groups nominated was extensive but the one that featured the most prominently was the SVP. Almost 10% of those responding to this particular question highlighted the SVP as the group that had most fostered in them a sense of the Gospel. Considered in the context of the total sample survey this represents 3% of all respondents, thus ranking the SVP as 6th overall (including those listed in figure 16) in terms of mediating the Gospel amongst those surveyed.

In response to the same question a wide range of religious orders were named. When grouped together these also represent 3% of all participants i.e. nearly 10% of those who answered this particular question. Other groups frequently mentioned include the Legion of Mary, Charismatic Renewal, Justice and Peace groups, Life and SPUC.

It is important, therefore, to understand that the answers outlined in figure 16 should be viewed with a mind to the other 30% of respondents who specified groups not listed in the question as having had a greater influence on them in terms of communicating the Gospel.

In relation to the impact of small groups in nurturing Gospel communities it is perhaps also interesting to discover that when asked in an earlier question about what builds fellowship in their parish (figure 5) 23% of respondents highlighted the contribution of 'house groups' (i.e. for prayer, Bible study etc.) and 1.5% of people mentioned the contribution of groups with a pattern or rule of life such as Cursillo and Focolare.

Lay formation

The aim of questions related to formation was to try to gain an impression of the extent to which parishioners are actively involved in mission and ministry within their local church and to determine the degree to which they have been equipped for such roles in the form of training and support.

It is clear from figure 17 that there are two predominant roles in the parish performed by those questioned. Namely, that of reading and that of being a eucharistic minister. The majority of other roles listed each account for between 20-25% of respondents, bearing in mind that many respondents may be involved in more than one area of parish ministry. What is perhaps more notable is the comparatively lower proportion of those surveyed involved in youth ministry (7.9%) and ministries possibly more peripheral to mainstream parish life such as 'lunch club, drop-in centre etc.' (3.7%).

It has been considered that some observers may be tempted to ascribe certain stereotypical characteristics to the survey population by virtue of the fact that up to half of all participants are eucharistic ministers or readers, the implication being that it is likely that 50% of respondents were 'recruited' for the survey from amongst what might be deemed to be a 'core' group of active parishioners, which is to be found in most parishes. Hence, one might tend to view the survey sample as an unrealistic representation of the target population.

However, it is helpful to bear in mind that the remit of the research was largely to question those active in faith and in parish ministry as to how they have been evangelised and how

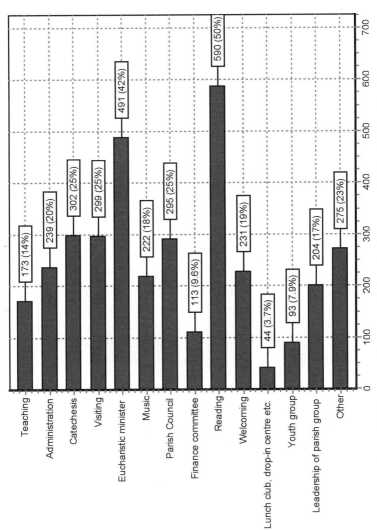

Figure 17: Do you perform any of the roles in your parish that is listed here?

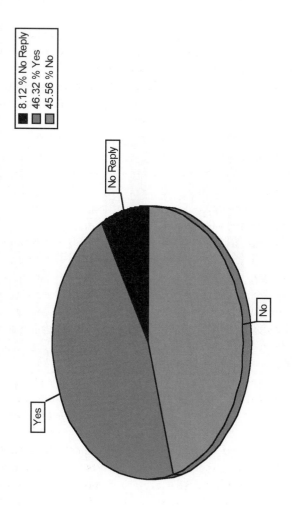

8.12 % No Reply
46.32 % Yes
45.56 % No

No Reply

No

Yes

Figure 18: Have you been given any training in relation to the work you do in your parish?

they are fulfilling their baptismal call to service in the context of taking a full and active role in the service of their local church. Hence, the responses might be considered to add more rather than less weight of evidence as to how and where evangelisation has been most effective in terms of the range and variety of factors that have influenced participants. It is also important to be mindful that an equal number of participants do not appear, by implication, to fall into the category of 'core' parishioners and so the sample is balanced.

When questioned as to whether they had received any training for the role they perform in the parish (figure 18) equal numbers of participants responded in the affirmative and the negative (46% in each case). One might be tempted to conclude from this that a large number of parishioners have received some kind of formation for ministry. However, it seems more likely that such a response is in large part a reflection of the fact that 42% of respondents to the previous question (figure 17) are eucharistic ministers for which training is mandatory.

Equally, this might suggest that of the 46% of respondents who claim to have received training 42% are eucharistic ministers. Hence, there are, by implication, only about 4% of participants involved in other parish ministries who claim to have had any training for the task they perform. In other words, it would appear to be a strong possibility that amongst those responding to this survey there has been virtually no training for other roles that people perform in the parish.

The respondents who had received no training for the roles they perform were asked to specify what forms of training or support (if any) would meet their needs (figure 18). The most frequent requests were for training in relation to youth ministry, liturgy (music and children's liturgy), catechesis and basic doctrine. There were some heartfelt requests for more and better communication with parish clergy and concern over issues to do with child protection was mentioned by a considerable number of participants.

In connection with the question of training for collaborative lay ministry it is also instructive to examine some of the responses from questions addressed specifically to professional

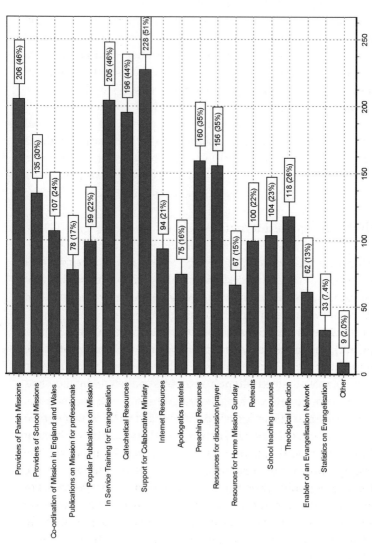

Figure 19: What would you most wish for from an 'Agency for Evangelisation' sponsored by the Bishops' Conference?

workers in the field of evangelisation, of whom parish priests were the largest constituency surveyed. They were asked to indicate what their priorities would be in terms of the activities of a new 'Agency for Evangelisation'.

The responses illustrated in figure 19 suggest that the single highest priority for evangelisation in the minds of the majority of parish professionals is for collaborative ministry. It is interesting to note that only slightly subsidiary to this is an appeal for providers of parish missions (46%) and in-service training (46%) as contributions to evangelisation.

> The most urgent factor is lay collaboration and lay training in my opinion.
>
> *Respondent in PP survey*

What has ignited a sense of the Gospel?

Participants in each of the surveys were asked a number of questions directly related to their own personal experience of evangelisation in an attempt to determine the range and variety of ways in which evangelisation takes place.

Participants were asked to respond to each element of this question on a scale from 'not at all' to 'extremely so' in terms of the impact of each factor on them personally in relation to their experience of evangelisation. Hence, the results are detailed and appear quite complex when illustrated (figure 20).

It is very clear from figure 20 that the means by which people are most effectively evangelised rely predominantly on human relationships and pastoral care. This is evidenced by the strongly affirmative responses in elements relating to the influence of family, friends, having children, marriage, times of personal crisis and the sacrament of reconciliation. There are also very positive responses in areas related to personal study and reflection such as retreats, Bible study, reading scripture and preaching.

Factors which seem to have a particularly low impact in communicating the Gospel include (in order of least

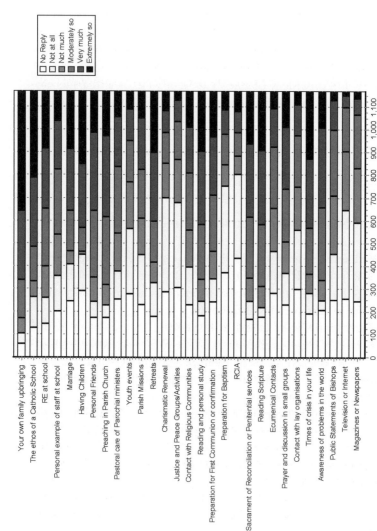

Figure 20: To what extent have the following ignited a sense of the gospel?

importance) RCIA, preparation for baptism, Charismatic Renewal, Justice and Peace, television and the internet, magazines and newspapers, youth events and contact with lay organisations.

Given the age structure of the sample some of these responses are perhaps predictable. For instance, one would not anticipate a sample of whom 50% of respondents are aged 50+ to have the a great deal of direct experience of baptism preparation, RCIA and youth events which have become much more prevalent in the Church relatively recently.

What brings people into deeper Christian activity?

Figure 21 is revealing in relation to understanding how important participants perceive certain factors to have been in their initial and ongoing encounter with the Gospel. What is very apparent yet again, is that it is in the context of the family that faith would seem to be most effectively communicated and nurtured. Secondary to this influence is the importance attached to a sense of belonging in the local Church, which was mentioned by 67% of participants.

Equally, factors related to the experience of worship and personal devotions are very influential in the mediation and enrichment of faith. For instance, half of all respondents attribute a sense of personal encounter with God as having an impact on their faith development.

The importance of schools is again prevalent, more than half of all the participants indicating that this was an area of significant influence on them in terms of encounter with the Gospel and of considerably more impact than the influence of friends and preaching.

At the other end of the scale what is perhaps most notable is the poor response in relation to personal invitation as an effective instrument for evangelisation in the experience of those surveyed. This would seem to be significant, not least when considered in the context of other findings, which

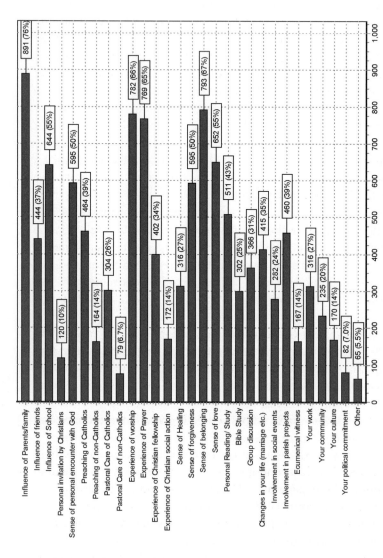

Figure 21: Which of these helped you personally come to or enrich your faith?

highlight the primacy of personal relationships in communicating the Gospel.

In summary, the majority of respondents attribute familial relationships and a sense of belonging allied to experience of worship and personal devotions as the most effective means by which they have encountered the Gospel. Factors having least impact in mediating the Gospel to the majority of respondents include the care of non-Catholics, political commitment and personal invitations by Christians.

Whilst, on the one hand, the results appear to paint a particularly optimistic picture regarding the influence of family in relation to embracing the Gospel, such a situation is, on the other hand, disconcerting in the light of predicted trends in Church demographics, since it is precisely this primary influence of family as a contribution to evangelisation that is likely to be lost at an increasing rate in the coming years. Yet again, this raises serious questions in relation to the future vitality of the Church and the evangelisation of young people in particular.

'Justice and Peace' and other diaconal measures

From a possible five equally weighted choices per respondent 90% cited worship as one of the areas where most energy is directed in the parish (figure 22). Over half of all respondents believed pastoral care (55%), and parish schools (53%), to be amongst the activities where most energy is directed in their parish while 45% indicated likewise for sacramental programmes.

At the opposing end of the scale activities where considerably less energy was felt to be devoted include community engagement (11%), confronting injustice (11%), serving neighbours (13%) and learning together (13%).

Such comparatively low responses for activities related to service, community involvement and working for social change, as opposed to the apparent commitment to worship, schools and pastoral care, tends towards creating an impression of a very insular and self-serving parish environment. This

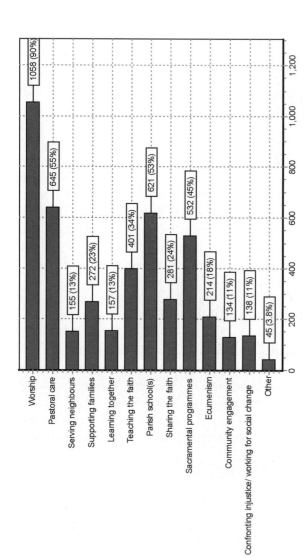

Figure 22: Where do you think most energy goes in your parish?

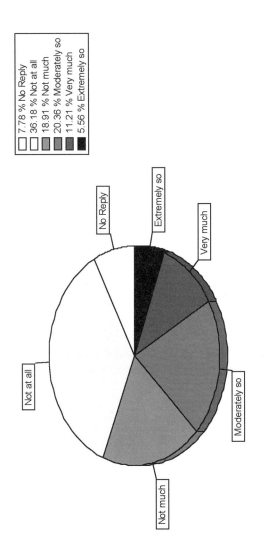

Figure 23: Extent of involvement in action for justice/community service organised or supported by parish.

impression is perhaps given added weight by responses to questions (below) directed at action for justice or service to the broader community beyond the parish.

The largest response to the question in figure 23 in any single category was in the negative, whereby over a third of those questioned claimed to have no involvement at all in parish supported initiatives for social action/justice and peace. Including the 'not much' respondents this proportion rises to 55% of those surveyed. Including 'no reply' respondents, 63% of those questioned had no apparent sustained involvement in parish supported service of the community within and/or beyond the parish. 37% of those questioned claim to be engaged in some parish-based activity for justice/community action.

The vast majority of respondents when questioned about their involvement in action for justice in the community beyond their parish would claim to have no engagement at all (69%, figure 24). Hence, it would appear that not only do most respondents have little commitment to action for social justice within their parish but that such a stance is not counterbalanced by action in the broader community. Indeed those questioned seem less likely to be involved in service to the broader community outside the parish (25%) than they would be inclined to be within the broader parish context (37%). Such findings seem to beg the question as to the extent to which the local church is being 'Good News' to the broader community in which it is set.

When asked about important social and global issues (figure 25), 39% of respondents felt that their parish had a moderate degree of concern whilst over one quarter felt that there was little or no apparent such concern demonstrated in their parish (27% including 'no reply').

> We talk a lot about marginalised people, but seem to think that including them in bidding prayers is enough.
> *Respondent to general survey*

The remaining 34% of those questioned felt that their parish was very concerned with important social/global issues. This possibly suggests a general perception amongst those surveyed that there is a moderate level of

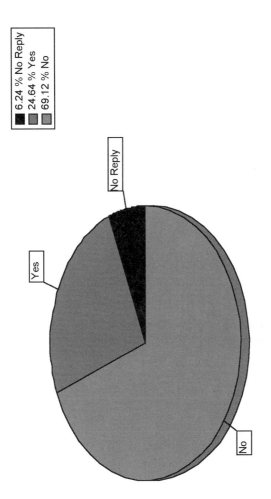

Figure 24: Are you involved in Action for justice beyond your parish?

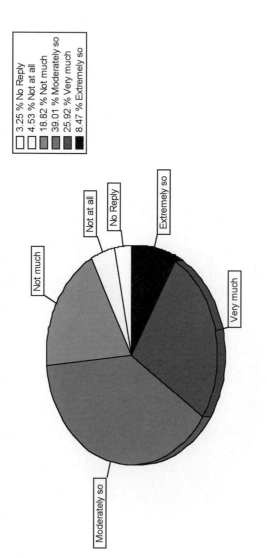

Figure 25: How much is your parish concerned with important social/global issues?

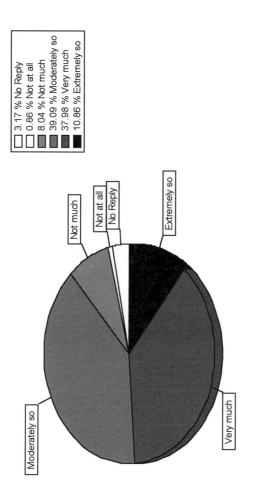

Figure 26: How much is the wider Church concerned with important social/global issues?

genuine concern within their parishes for 'social / global issues' but that (by virtue of their response to previous questions) many of the respondents are not personally disposed to put such concerns into action in the context of service to the wider community (see figures 22, 23 and 24).

49% of those questioned credit the 'wider Church' with having a high degree of concern for social / global issues (compared with 34% for the parish), whilst 8% felt that the wider Church showed 'not much' commitment to such issues (figure 26). The responses to this question are in some contrast to the same question asked of the parish. Almost three times as many respondents (23%) felt that the parish demonstrated no real concern for social / global issues.

This would seem to suggest something of a mismatch amongst those who were surveyed between perceptions of public exhortations to social action in the broader Church and practice at parish level.

Summary

The data as analysed thus far seem to indicate some key features of evangelisation in terms of how it is understood and experienced and where and by what means the Gospel is most readily communicated. By contrast and by omission the data also seem to point to areas of concern in terms of locations where the Gospel is not being as effectively commended.

What seems consistently apparent from the data in their entirety is that there is a diversity of means by which evangelisation takes place. Amongst these it is clear, however, that the majority of people receive the Gospel in a gradual rather than a sudden way. Many of the results outlined in this section indicate that personal relationships are the most influential factor in communicating the Gospel as opposed to the impact of dramatic experiences or large events.

These findings are supported by recent ecumenical research, which suggests that most people are evangelised gradually and not as the result of a sudden decision or experience. This is held to be especially true for young people.[140] There are some obvious implications following from this, notably: if most people are on a gradual journey there is a clear, if not urgent, need to find methods of evangelising that fit into this pattern. This does not suggest that the potential for sudden conversions should be ruled out but that there is a need for a diversity of approaches to evangelisation which are weighted accordingly in the application of approaches, vehicles and instruments.

Responses in all aspects of the research suggest that the single highest priority for evangelisation in the minds of those surveyed is support for collaborative ministry. It is interesting to note that only slightly subsidiary to this is an appeal for providers of parish missions, in-service training and the desire for various tangible resources.

> There is clearly a great need to evangelise the attending community first, i.e. to put a fire in their belly for the Gospel. Presently there is a great lack of a basic appreciation of ecclesiology. What is mission? What is authority? What is collaboration?
> *Respondent to survey of seminary students*

As to the locations of evangelisation, it is clear that the majority of respondents believe the Gospel to be most effectively enacted in the liturgy of the Eucharist. Indeed, the data more generally suggests a deep desire to be nourished by the Word of God through such things as the celebration of the sacraments, retreats, Bible study, faith sharing and other related activities. In contrast, there would appear to be considerably more reluctance to share what has been received in the form of witness to and service of the Gospel in the wider community. The implication is that many are happy to receive the Good News but less so to communicate it to others!

> I have a great sense of belonging to my parish which is a very active parish with lay people taking on most ministries. However, I

---

[140] See John Finney in *Finding Faith Today: How Does It Happen?* (British and Foreign Bible Society, Swindon, 1994), p. 25.

feel that we minister to each other (Mass attenders) rather than
the wider community.

Respondent to general survey

The benevolent interpretation of this picture might be that
there is again a prevailing sense amongst Catholics in England
of Wales of being planted in 'alien soil'. Or, more precisely, that
there is a prevailing sense of being situated within a broader
culture (secular, materialistic etc.) that is inhospitable to the
Gospel and that consequently engenders a crisis of confidence
in those responsible for spreading the 'Good News' and makes
them feel inadequate to the task. If so, the implication would be
that the Catholic community generally requires resourcing and
training for the task. The less generous interpretation would be
that many are heedless of their baptismal call to evangelisation
and its implications in terms of the lay vocation.

In any case, the general picture which emerges from the
research is one of a rather insular Church in the local context
which seems more concerned to 'look after its own' rather than
having a concern for evangelising the broader community. An
important question emerges as to the role of evangelisation in
bringing critical faculties to bear on 'belonging' in a parochial
setting. Other questions worthy of note which the research does
not address directly might include the whole area of obstacles to
evangelisation and the factors that make people choose not to
belong to the Church. In other words, this research is limited in
its scope and it may be instructive to consider what the 'missing
data' might suggest.

7. Locations of evangelisation

Given the above, it seems sensible to consider a number of models or, perhaps better, locations of evangelisation. The following short notes are intended to place some possibilities for evangelisation and some initiatives. There is a danger that these are seen as independent 'stand alone', even contradictory activities: in fact they are complementary and should be thought of as overlapping rather than compartmentalised.

Presence

Prayer and sacrament

The visible life of the Church itself and her/our presence in the world must be considered the starting point of evangelisation. This is more than simply a pragmatic necessity, it is a theological imperative. God in Christ has chosen to use the Church as a privileged partner in his purposes of love for the world. Therefore the Church must herself be constantly open to the Gospel, so that her illumination by the Good News of Jesus can become a beacon in the world. The primary location of this illumination must be prayer and worship.

> Evangelisation to me is locating the Spirit of God in others and entering into a dialogue - Spirit to Spirit. This cannot be fruitful unless prayer is the fundamental constituént of one's spiritual life. Teaching/helping people to deepen prayer life and see its fundamental importance is number one.
> *Respondent to PP survey*

The conciliar insight that the liturgy of the Eucharist is the 'source and summit'[141] of Christian life must apply to Evangelisation. The presence of the Church as a worshipping sacramental community is both the springboard for evangelisation and the achievement of evangelisation. At the Eucharist, in being drawn to the Triune God by grace and

---

[141] Vatican II, *Sacrosanctum Concilium* 10 and *Lumen Gentium* 11.

responding in prayer and praise, the Christian assembly is most fully herself on earth. It is therefore right to begin a survey of patterns and locations of evangelisation with the Eucharist. It is here that the people of God are nourished with the Word of Life and the sacraments of salvation and are therefore themselves constantly re-evangelised. The sacramental and praying community is the *sine qua non* of evangelisation: the Church is called to become Good News in order to share Good News and to receive those who have responded to the Gospel. The celebration of the sacraments is in itself a missionary activity whereby the *Missio Dei* reveals itself to and through the People of God. The emphasis that many of our respondents gave to the centrality of liturgy echoes this. More than this the prayer and closeness to the Lord that lie at the heart of the eucharistic celebration are the bedrock of holiness - perhaps the most attractive and authentic quality that the Church can seek.

However, it must also be noted that there are other ways of worship beyond the Mass, and that the Mass itself can be inappropriate as a vehicle of making the Gospel accessible to those who have not yet been initiated into the eucharistic assembly. There is a need for complementary forms of worship which can celebrate in an inclusive way the workings of grace and the implicit and explicit faith of people. It is this celebrative aspect which has become the dominant thrust in many Catholic agencies of evangelisation, including the Catholic Missionary Society. The CMS mission process includes groups in parishes designing and implementing their own vision of non-eucharistic worship based around themes of their own choosing. This includes the choice of appropriate symbolic actions. Frequently this leads to much creativity and imagination as well as deep reflection on and commitment to the heart of the worship event. In some ways the freshness and communal ownership of worship this encapsulates has parallels with some aspects of the 'Alternative Worship' movement.[142]

---

[142] Cf. Mike Riddell, Mark Pierson and Cathy Kirkpartick, *The Prodigal Project* (SPCK, London, 2000).

Specific prayer for evangelisation should be a normal, indeed normative, part of Christian life in every parish and in every home. Every recitation of the Lord's Prayer is itself an evangelising prayer with its hallowing of God's name, the intercession for God's will to be done and for the kingdom to come and the benefits of God's love to be experienced. Further specific intercessory prayer that areas, neighbourhoods, streets and persons be transformed by the Gospel is both a readily achievable target and an evangelising activity well within the grasp of every Christian in every parish. Many parishes and individuals have committed themselves to regular prayer for evangelisation.

There are a wealth of occasions when those on the fringe and on the outside of the believing community may encounter the Church as a place of love and worship. We should therefore include in this evangelistic ministry of prayerful presence such things as school Masses and school assemblies, baptism, first communion, marriage and funerals. That is not to say that these need to be distorted from their primary purpose into exercises in salesmanship but rather that their primary purpose of being when a community gathers before God, receives from God and gives back to God should be a moment when all present are made welcome and can glimpse something of the love of God in his Church.

Wordless witness
Evangelii Nuntiandi uses the happy phrase 'Wordless witness' to describe how a Christian presence can transform society.

> Above all the Gospel must be proclaimed by witness. Take a Christian or a handful of Christians who, in the midst of their own community, show their capacity for understanding and acceptance, their sharing of life and destiny with other people, their solidarity with the efforts of all for whatever is noble and good. Let us suppose that, in addition, they radiate in an altogether simple and unaffected way their faith in values that go beyond current values, and their hope in something that is not seen and that one would not dare to imagine. Through this

wordless witness these Christians stir up irresistible questions in the hearts of those who see how they live: Why are they like this? Why do they live in this way? What or who is it that inspires them? Why are they in our midst? Such a witness is already a silent proclamation of the Good News and a very powerful and effective one. Here we have an initial act of evangelization. The above questions will ask, whether they are people to whom Christ has never been proclaimed, or baptized people who do not practice, or people who live as nominal Christians but according to principles that are in no way Christian, or people who are seeking, and not without suffering, something or someone whom they sense but cannot name. Other questions will arise, deeper and more demanding ones, questions evoked by this witness which involves presence, sharing, solidarity, and which is an essential element, and generally the first one, in evangelization. All Christians are called to this witness, and in this way they can be real evangelizers.[143]

One is reminded of the dictum attributed to St Francis of Assisi, 'Preach the Gospel always: use words only when necessary.'[144] This is also reminiscent of aspects of the so-called 'Tentmaker ministries' proposed by some Evangelical groups.[145]

[143] *Evangelii Nuntiandi* 21.

[144] This notion is developed in the document *A Spirituality of Work* by the Committee for the World of Work of the Bishops' Conference (Catholic Media Trust, 2001, p. 37). This tag is quoted in several forms and attributed to St. Francis of Assisi but we have yet to trace it within the Saint's writings. However, it seems within the spirit of St. Francis and consistent with texts such as *The Little Flowers of St. Francis*, ch. 50: 'But as for me, I desire this privilege from the Lord, that never may I have any privilege from man, except to do reverence to all, and to convert the world by obedience to the Holy Rule rather by example than by word.' (tr. T. Okey, Everyman, 1951, p. 295).

[145] E.g. Jonathan Lewis (ed.), *Working your way to the nations: a guide to effective tentmaking* (William Carey Library, Pasadena, CA, 1993), or {www.tentmaking.org}. It is worth noting that the language of 'tentmaking' has at least two dynamics. The first is associated with those who gain access into secular or non-Christian societies because of their skills and work and thus can evangelise in that secular or non-

Life lived in the Gospel communicates the Gospel to others. The success of Steve Redgrave, now Sir Stephen, encouraged the highest interest ever in people wanting to take up rowing as a sport in the UK: it was seeing his actions which touched and attracted people. Likewise Christian lives lived with holiness, fidelity, joy, love and compassion are attractive. Further, this witness of life is something that every Christian is called to. We talk of the responsibility of evangelisation belonging to every Christian: here is an opportunity for every Christian. In addition, the wordless witness of each Christian has the power to show something of the Gospel into every home, every school, every workplace, every social encounter, every pub and club, every gym and sports field, and every other place of human activity. This is why the 'synthesis of faith and life' - the application of the Gospel to and integration of the Gospel within all aspects of daily life is so important for evangelisation. Lives and lifestyles can be more eloquent than homilies.

To be sure the Apostolic Exhortation continues to say that such 'wordless witness' is not enough alone and that there needs to be explicit explanation and

> People who really believe they have 'Good News' to share don't need a reason or to be told to do it: they just do it quite naturally. We need Catholics to realise that 'evangelisation' does not mean one has to go out to 'convert' people in the old sense, but to let others see why one can have this same experience of life today with all its pressures and difficulties - and yet be someone of commonsense, joy, hope and glad to be alive because God really *is*; and he loves me and always will.
> *Respondent to PP survey*

Christian world, and the second is the development of Christian ministers in secular employment as a way of bringing skills and resources into the Christian community (and thereby being able to afford ministry in the Church). These may well be complementary aspects of the same thing. At this juncture we would emphasis the value of the former as the reaching out of the Christian community into the world. Insights into the latter may be found in James M. Francis and Leslie J. Francis, *Tentmaking: Perspectives on self-supporting ministry* (Gracewing, London, 1998).

proclamation of Christ and the faith of the Church in him (*Evangelii Nuntiandi* 22). Yet we should acknowledge that the foundation upon which authentic proclamation can genuinely proceed is a life lived in Christ which both concretely enacts the Gospel and inspires existential questions in others.

A particular example of this is the witness given by 'Peer Ministry' among young people. It has been noted that young people sharing their experiences of faith with other young people is a powerful witness. Diocesan youth centres, diocesan youth teams and other groups often give young people with relatively inactive faith the chance to encounter other young people with active faith. As such these are opportunities to challenge young people with the demands of the Gospel by the demonstration of the joy and liveliness of Christian living.

Visible parish

The parish itself needs to be visible. There are many messages given out from the parish by what those outside the parish see of it. The state of buildings, notice boards, the contents of notice boards and the profile of the community in its neighbourhood give messages which are both subliminal and preliminal. That is to say they both enter into the unverbalised knowledge of people about that ecclesial community and either assist people to enter into it (enable them to cross the threshold (*limina*)) or deter them.

This visibility is closely associated with vitality. The more vital the parish is, the more it is naturally visible. Just as there is a personal attractiveness in the life of individual Christians, so should there be an attractiveness in our shared communal life. There is a need for Christians to enjoy their life of faith. The delight in being God's people communicates itself in a way that dogmatic statements never can. One of the ecumenical partners interviewed for this research noted that what he found attractive about the Catholic Church was that it was a place where 'you could have a good time'. (Although he also challenged us as being a Church in which we 'could get away with things'.) The strength of Catholic pleasure in our human, social, cultural and artistic life should not be underestimated -

Christianity can be fun - even if this needs to be married with an awareness to guard against complacency and indifference.

> Need to include an element of enjoying what is being done, not just duty.
> *Respondent to PP survey*

Within such visibility we should include Church advertising, leafleting campaigns giving information about Church activities (e.g. delivery of a welcome leaflet to newly built houses in a parish), engagement of the parish in its neighbourhood, in ecumenical fora and in the structures of civil society. (Some of the latter will be further discussed in terms of *diakonia* below.) Certainly one of the features of the parish missions observed by the Sion Community, Redemptorists and CMS was that all encouraged the parishes they worked with to present themselves, to name what they did and produce materials which showed what they did (e.g. parish exhibitions, posters etc.)

'Celtic model'

There have been of late several recoveries and reinventions of Celtic spiritualities, and to a lesser extent a revival of interest in Anglo-Saxon ecclesiastic structures and spirituality. The history of the establishment of Christianity in these islands by both Celtic and Anglo-Saxon pioneers may provide pointers for contemporary evangelisation. These may suggest a special understanding of evangelisation as presence. Some would stress a Celtic model of evangelisation based on a reading of history in which dedicated communities settled with a people and identified with them entering into the cultural frame and experiences of non-believers. Similar emphases in a Roman/Anglo-Saxon millieu, prefiguring current debates on inculturation, may be found in the advice Gregory the Great gave to Augustine of Canterbury via Mellitus:

> When, therefore, Almighty God shall bring you to the most reverend Bishop Augustine, our brother, tell him what I have, upon mature deliberation on the affair of the English, determined upon, *viz.*, that the temples of the idols in that nation ought not to be destroyed; but let the idols that are in

them be destroyed; let holy water be made and sprinkled in the said temples, let altars be erected, and relics placed. For if those temples are well built, it is requisite that they be converted from the worship of devils to the service of the true God; that the nation, seeing that their temples are not destroyed, may remove error from their hearts, and knowing and adoring the true God, may the more familiarly resort to the places to which they have been accustomed.[146]

To use the familiar and customary as doorways into the Christian seems as wise today as it was then. It is good to recall that early Christian communities did try to relate in a respectful way to the communities in which they were set. Thus Celtic monastic communities lived deep lives of compassion and prayer and practised hospitality. As such this approach would emphasise imagination, music, poetry and storytelling, relationships, conversations and actions above didactic words and propositions.[147]

Three aspects of this resonate with contemporary Catholic evangelisation. First is that people today need witnesses more than teachers. Secondly, that the way into faith involves building friendships and community and not simply convincing people of arguments. Rather, points of contact need to be made with people's experiences. Initiatives which may demonstrate aspects of this include both the RCIA and the Alpha Course. Thirdly, this underlines the need for dedicated communities which may be in a complementary relationship to existing parishes. (Part of Finney's argument is that the 'Roman' model of dioceses and parishes works better for maintaining 'Christendom' whereas Celtic monasticism worked better in the

---

[146] Recorded in Bede, *Ecclesiastical History of the English Nation*, book I, ch. 30.

[147] The Anglican John Finney has presented several of these ideas as ways of the contemporary Church learning from the sixth century evangelisation of these islands in his *Recovering the Past: Celtic and Roman Mission* (DLT, London, 1996). See also the American Evangelical, George G. Hunter, *The Celtic Way of Evangelism: How Christianity Can Reach the West ... Again* (Abingdon Press, Nashville, 2000).

circumstances of 'Paganism'.) The work of the Northumberland Community, the Pilgrims Community, Cor-Lumen Christi and other 'new movements' may demonstrate this, as well as the continuing witness of other more established lay associations, religious communities and societies of apostolic life.

Direct initial kerygmatic proclamation

Individual (one-to-one) initiatives - informal
There is little doubt that most people come to faith through the influence of family, friends and their social network. Because the nature of such natural friendships are informal, and hence not consciously organised, they can be forgotten. It is through genuine and organic relationships that the faith is caught rather than taught. Faith surely should be contagious. Contact with Christians should be in itself the deepest communication of the Gospel. Our research shows a high percentage of active Catholics attribute their sense of the Gospel to their families and personal friendships. However, they need supporting and equipping. Resourcing the domestic Church to assist families raise their children in the faith must be a priority. Equipping men, women and children with confidence to integrate their faith into their lives and to share their experience of faith is essential. Lay formation must be the cornerstone of a missionary church.

Families and households, friends, colleagues and neighbours have always been a natural place for proclaiming the *kerygma*. This is both a pattern from the New Testament (cf. Cornelius, Acts 10), from the early evangelisation of England and Wales (cf. the conversion of royal households) to the present day. This may be called a form of *oikos* (or *oikia*[148]) evangelisation - the spread of the Gospel through a network of relationships and personal

---

[148] Both these Greek words are used in the New Testament to refer to house and household, and both are used in the contemporary discussion on evangelisation through social networks although the first is the more common.

spheres of influence.[149] Our purpose here is not to recommend any particular scheme but to stress the principle that human relationships between Christians and their families, friends and neighbours are the most powerful evangelising force in England and Wales. Indeed, although we shall note the possibilities and potential of some more formal organisation below, we feel that the natural informal network is in itself a vehicle of evangelisation. Ecumenical research has shown that family and friends are the overwhelmingly most influential factor in bringing people to faith. Indeed, of the Catholic participants (recently initiated adults through RCIA), 36 percent said that their girlfriend/boyfriend/spouse was the main factor in them joining the Church.[150] (Although one friendly non-Catholic consultant to this research has observed that the lack of welcome of a non-Catholic partner during preparation for a Catholic marriage was in that specific case detrimental to the Christian commitment of both husband and spouse.) Our research shows that most respondents listed family and friends as significant in passing on to them a sense of the Gospel.

Individual (one-to-one) initiatives - formal

Such *oikos* evangelisation as described in the previous section may be assisted with some focussed preparation. Formal courses such as Alpha or 'Come and See' may assist, as may cell groups into which friends, families and neighbours can be

---

[149] This use of the term *oikos* has become influential amongst Evangelicals, cf. Win Arn and Charles Arn, *The Master's Plan for Making Disciples* (Grand Rapids: Baker, 1997) and Win Arn, 'The Genius behind early church growth can be discovered in your Church' in Glenn C. Smith (ed.), *Evangelizing Adults* (Paulist National Catholic Evangelization, Washington and Tyndale House, Wheaton, Illinois, 1985), and has been promoted amongst Catholics in this country by, amongst others, the Sion Community. See also Michael Hurley *Transforming Your Parish: Building a Faith Community* (Columba Press, Blackrock, Dublin, 1998) for a parish based working out of *oikos* evangelisation through the 'Come and See' course and the establishment of cell groups.

[150] John Finney, *Finding Faith Today: How does it happen?* (British and Foreign Bible Society, London, 1992) p. 36f., percentage on p. 39.

comfortably included.[151] This may include practice in naming what difference it is that the Gospel has made in the Christian's life and telling their faith stories. RCIA sponsorship, parish faith sharing discussion groups and other occasions can give people confidence in this area. There are also more formal opportunities for people to share faith individually and to be given training in living their Christian missionary vocation in their social networks. We came across several visiting schemes, prayer partnerships and neighbouring initiatives. We were aware of the 'Friendship Evangelism' associated with Evangelism Explosion and of the suspicions that these techniques have aroused. However, we were not able to see direct equivalents in the Catholic Church. The 'Schools of Evangelisation' promoted by the Pilgrims Community, the Sion Community and others follow different models but are clearly providing people with more formal training and tools with which to approach their friends and neighbours. These include training in a 'core Gospel' - a series of statements to be presented to those outside the Church - such as God loves you, sin separates us from God, Jesus offers a way past sin to eternal life, and each person must choose to accept or reject this offer.[152] However, only a very small number of respondents considered these significant in their experience.

We have already considered visiting in terms of raising parish profiles. It is also to be noted that most parishes formally engaged in 'Mission Weeks' include a commitment to visiting and accompaniment with the particular purpose of inviting fringe, seekers, unchurched, dechurched etc., to come to Mission Services. Many avenues of invitation have been observed from letters delivered to parents by children at Catholic schools, door to door visiting with personal invitations, parish mailings to radio, newspaper and other media invitations, and more. The imagination and sensitivity shown in such exercises is to be commended. Different evangelisation

---

[151] See Hurley, *Transforming Your Parish* (1998).

[152] From Sion Evangelisation Centre for National Training, *Pass it on*. The Pilgrims Community would present a related six point scheme.

agencies do have different approaches to such visiting: e.g. The Sion Community have a visiting week with a trained visiting team coming into the parish whereas the CMS asks parishioners to organise a group within the parish to achieve similar aims.

Spiritual direction or counselling opportunities

Discussion with several groups has pointed out the deep individual work done in the field of spiritual direction and counselling. This is an open-ended person centred dialogue within which 'Good News' is discerned.

Although many practitioners would not immediately see such activity as proclamation, clearly such processes of discernment contribute to personal, and even social, transformation.

One perceived need that this approach keys in to is the view that what is needed today is not more religion but deeper spirituality.

The use of gifts

Since every Christian has the right and duty to evangelise,[153] we should presume that their baptismal apostolate includes appropriate gifts for the task. Thus the various skills, powers of imagination and commitment of each member of the Church should be celebrated and each should feel that they have a contribution to make to the work of evangelisation. Many of the gifts graced upon members of every parish can contribute to direct initial proclamation: these may include gifts of music, art, imagination, social skills, organisational skills as well as those perhaps considered more immediately evangelistic such as public speaking or sharing testimony. The breadth of gifts inherent in our people should match the width of the task before us.

Part of the Good News we have received and desire to share is that every person is valuable and precious to God and can contribute to the continuation of the mission of Christ in the Church. Working together so that the gifts of God graced upon

---

[153] See above p. 48f.

each Christian may be used for the proclamation and enactment of the Gospel must be stressed in contemporary evangelisation. Collaborative ministry is not an optional extra, but a necessity of being Church.[154]

However, there must also be noted a more specific use of spiritual gifts in evangelisation. We have met some who have used charismatic gifts in evangelisation and others who have been influenced strongly by experiencing such use. While we judge that this is unusual in Catholic evangelisation, we also feel that we should report it.

Individual media driven initiatives: videos, websites, poster campaigns etc.

Several agencies have produced material addressed to enquirers. The Catholic Enquiry Office continues to produce material to be given free to those wishing to know more about the faith with new material, *Living Faith Stories* and *Living Faith*, launched in 2001. In the 1990s the CEO on average sent out just over 3,000 sets of free books each year. Since the launch

> For many [the proclamation given by the availability of books and other publications about the good news of Jesus] would naturally be a first step ... before seeking contact with an individual or parish. *Respondent to general survey*

of the new books in July last year, 1,287 copies have been sent out. Websites have been set up with evangelising and apologetic materials.[155] Many parishes have produced their own websites which not only give information about the parish but often include explicitly evangelistic information and invitations.

The film *The Miracle Maker* attracted much attention and several Catholic parishes organised visits to see it. The 'Jesus' video is one specific example of an international media initiative in the Jubilee Year. Millions of copies of this were distributed in Rome during the Holy Year Jubilee celebrations.

---

[154] *The Sign We Give*.
[155] E.g. {www.cms.org.uk/ceo}, {www.pilgrimscommunity.com} and {www.cor-lumenchristi.org}.

Large Group events: Mission week or weekend (cf. Crusade), Youth 2000

There exists in the Catholic psyche the notion of a Mission as an event. Two weeks, one week or a weekend of focussed happenings are seen as the 'Mission'. Several agencies arrange 'Celebration Weeks' (the language may vary), but most would express some concerns about being parachuted in to provide a show. Some researchers would suggest that 'Crusade' type large events are ineffective today. Indeed many of our ecumenical partners would share the feeling that large scale impersonal events are inappropriate for today.[156] However, there does remain a place for evangelistic events, particularly at the parochial and local level.

As we shall consider below many agencies combine such event centred activities within the framework of a more extensive process.

It is worth giving special notice to the effectiveness of the retreats and festivals organised by Youth 2000,[157] not least because these do have a high profile among youth and young adults and were recorded as having a significant place in the fostering of vocations of seminarians. Also the opportunity is given for young people to evangelise young people and witness to their faith.

Small group initiatives

Modern men and women may find themselves more at home and welcome in the situation of a small group. This can be both personal and interactive. They can raise questions and develop personal relationships with others. Small groups enable faith-sharing to happen in a natural and unthreatening way which deepens encounter with the Gospel and the community created by the Gospel. RCIA has the capacity to provide just such an ambience where issues can be explored and faith shared. However, there may be a tension here: often RCIA catechetics,

---

[156] Cf. Robert Warren, *Signs of Life: how goes the decade of evangelism?* (Church House Publishing for the General Synod of the Church of England, London, 1996), pp. 50-52.

[157] See {www.youth2000.org}.

for very good reasons and building on sound theology and pastoral priorities, lays the stress on people reflecting on their life experiences in the company of a learning community. As such some would suggest that it may not sufficiently give weight to direct initial kerygmatic proclamation. Indeed many prefer to describe the early steps of RCIA as 'enquiry' rather than 'evangelisation' - although the two titles are necessary complements in the process.

> Evangelisation starts with welcome - making people feel comfortable in the presence of Christians. It is important to start where people are - with what is important to them. In small faith sharing groups one can journey with others deeper into Jesus. Above all, people need to be and feel loved.
> *Respondent to general survey*

The Alpha Course has been both the most high profile and most successful recent initiative in establishing groups where issues of faith are discussed and the claims of Christ presented. The process of Alpha includes hospitality, a friendly meal, direct input and group discussion of that input. After a number of weeks it includes a session when participants may ask for the Holy Spirit to come into their lives. This combination has proved attractive in many Christian communities and has enabled many Catholics to become actively involved in kerygmatic proclamation in a non-threatening and natural way.

There have been criticisms of Alpha: that it is too individualistic, too conservative, too evangelical, too simple, too charismatic, lacking a sacramental understanding of the Church, too much aimed at a middle-class audience, or too didactic. However, it is also a package which is within the reach of most parishes and which has proven itself to be beneficial for many and has empowered many Catholics in becoming active agents of evangelisation. Such effectiveness in promoting faith decisions and enabling Christians to minister to those outside the Church should be applauded. Certainly it needs follow up: both the other video series prepared by Catholic Evangelisation Services and the RCIA can build upon any faith decisions catalysed by Alpha.

A further example of evangelisation through small groups are meetings in people's homes. This can be related to the *oikos* evangelisation considered above. It is the creation of a non-threatening environment in which friends and neighbours can share in the life of the Church without undue pressure. Often such groups are formed for what might be considered internal Church purposes - prayer, Bible study and so forth - but they contain an opportunity for others to enter into the life of faith.

Communities and movements

We have already introduced the part that communities and movements play in evangelisation and we shall consider the role of communites further below as we consider *koinonia*. However, it is important to record here that those who have been committed to *koinonia* often live out their common life in *kerygma*. An important set of examples of this are those New Communities and Movements for whom the call to a New Evangelisation has become an essential part of their identity and apostolate.

One important example to consider again in this context is Youth 2000.[158] Although not perhaps in a formal sense a community, it is a movement drawn together for the specific purpose of evangelisation. It was formed as a response to the call of John Paul II for New Evangelisation and for young people to be the 'Saints of the New Millennium'. Youth 2000 would see itself as a gateway into the Church. Within its prayer groups, festivals and retreats it offers young people a clear and simple presentation of the Gospel backed up with personal testimonies, lively music, extended eucharistic adoration, recitation of the rosary and the sacrament of reconciliation. From the gateway of Youth 2000 many young people have made Christian commitments including impressive numbers of seminarians and vocations to various forms of religious life.

---

[158] {www.youth2000.org}.

Seeker services

We are aware that some Christian traditions have made much of worship opportunities particularly aimed at the unchurched and those on the fringe of Christian commitment. Such 'seeker services' have been promoted by movements such as Willow Creek. Some Catholics have engaged in similar services: one example would be those organised by Cor-Lumen Christi. Indeed, they make up one element of the traditional parish mission - although may rarely these days be the staple diet of such a mission. Our research found some, but only a few, examples where Catholic parishes or other communities regularly offered worship whose primary audience was the unchurched or seekers.

Koinonia

Parish mission process(es)

Several evangelisation agencies are committed to processes of working with parishes in order to develop greater missionary activity within the parishes. Their contribution to evangelisation is therefore at the level of promoting *koinonia* or aspects of *mystagogia*. In particular, these flexible processes are intended to assist parishes discern their needs, develop confidence in lay ministry and collaborative patterns of working and enhance the evangelisation potential of local communities. One example is the Parish Development and Renewal process in the Archdiocese of Dublin.[159]

Similar principles and structures can be seen in the typical CMS parish or school mission process.[160] This process is again flexible and its structure dependent on the discernment and decision making of a particular local community. However, a

[159] See Dublin Diocesan Committee for Parish Development, *Parish Development and Renewal: Presenting the Dublin Experience* (Veritas, Dublin, 1993) and Donal Harrington (ed.), *Parish Renewal* vols. I and II (Columba, Blackrock, Dublin, 1997).

[160] See {www.cms.org.uk/strategy.htm}.

four stage process lasting nine to twelve months is common. Thus during this time of working with a parish CMS missioners accompany local people as they discover the mission needs of their community and develop and celebrate their faith and evangelisation. In the first stage, discernment is encouraged through meeting with the parish priest and others which leads to the creation of a 'Mission Team'. This group of twelve are focal to the process. They enter into a series of faith-sharing sessions in which they discern both their personal sources of faith and where the needs of their parish and local community may lie. These are then further rolled out to the wider parish so that several house groups can discuss the same issues using material provided by the CMS. The second stage is to develop that discernment by a series of groups organised around practical tasks in preparation for a Celebration Week. The themes, liturgies and all practical aspects of preparing for that week grow out of the parishioners with the CMS missioners offering some advice and guidance. As noted above, this collaborative approach to discerning themes, designing and implementing liturgies has often been one of the most powerful outcomes of the process. The third stage is the Celebration Week itself in which the people's faith is celebrated and their discernment expressed through a series of services at which the CMS missioners who have been accompanying them preside and preach at the liturgies prepared using the creativity, imagination and resources of the community. The fourth stage is the evaluation where the community can express what they have learned and plan for the future built upon their learnings. A parallel structure has been developed for work in schools.

Such process work is not about being parachuted in to deliver a mission for a parish or school, but is working with a local community to enable it to be missionary and foster the evangelisation ministries of those within that community. It is thus an act of evangelisation training through the mechanism of preparing for the celebration week. While the CMS currently has the most clearly developed process for such collaborative work in parishes and schools in England and Wales, the Sion

Community, the Redemptorists and others would also emphasise process elements and collaboration in their work with parishes.

Catechumenate

The recovered catechumenate is the structure the Church has provided for evangelisation. It must be given a strong emphasis as the theological and liturgical cornerstone for the presentation of the Gospel, encounter with the Gospel and growth in the Gospel. RCIA is perhaps at its strongest at building communities. The processes of reflecting on scripture, sharing faith experiences and building trust in a learning community enables those journeying together to grow in *koinonia*. RCIA is a powerful contribution to Christian formation working at many levels which go beyond just giving information about Christianity. It is a process which opens up Christian living both to catechists and sponsor and to catechumens and candidates.

We have had cause already to mention RCIA several times and it is worthwhile here to underline some of its powerful strengths in evangelisation:

- it is personal and interactive;
- it is liturgical;
- it enables encounter with scripture;
- it is communal;
- it builds relationships over time;
- it builds on experiences;
- it empowers people to articulate and share their faith experiences;
- it is tempting to describe it in management speak as SMART (Specific, Measurable, Achievable, Realistic, and has a Time-frame) - certainly the objectives of RCIA are feasible within any parish.

The further 'bonus' of RCIA is that it equips people to share their faith in a natural way. The conversations and encounters that happen in RCIA are open, exploratory dialogues in which people's life and faith experiences meet the scriptural traditions and the teachings of the Church. As such all involved (catechists, sponsors, enquirers, catechumens, candidates and neophytes) practise the skills of sharing what the Gospel means in their lives. This must have positive effects for the Church beyond the RCIA itself.

Core or covenant communities within ecclesial community

A particular focus for *koinonia* is the wide variety of communities distinct from but often contributing to parish life. Some communities set themselves up as seed bed communities within the wider community where people can live the Gospel in a dedicated manner, respond to charisms and have particular apostolates. Again we recall the long history of religious orders, societies of apostolic life and lay associations which have continually contributed to all aspects of evangelisation, often including within their charisms commitment to *kerygma*, *diakonia* and *koinonia*. Such communities remain active and contribute in many valuable ways to the life of the Church. Many of our respondents recognised the influence of these 'classic' forms of community life upon their own growth in the Gospel. Our consultations have shown that there has been significant growth in associate membership of communities which may reveal a new form of this expression of *koinonia*. We are also aware of new expressions of such 'classic' forms such as the Franciscan Friars of the Renewal, now establishing a house in East London, expressing their community life in service of the poor and working with Youth 2000 in direct initial kerygmatic proclamation.[161]

There has also been in recent years the rise of several new movements and new communities, again to some of whom we have already alluded. Certainly such movements have been given considerable support from the Pope and Magisterium, although we should also note substantial concerns.[162] Several of

[161] See {www.franciscanfriars.com} - their US home site, but with pages on the English house.

[162] Cf. *Novo Millennio Ineunte* 46. Also various interventions in the Extraordinary Synod. Note also the Report on the Neo-Catechumenate in Clifton Diocese, *Briefing* November 1996 and February 1997, and the insightful reflections of Jean Vanier on 'New Lay Movements', *Briefing* April 1997.

these have eagerly adopted the call for a 'New Evangelisation'. While we judge that their present size and influence in England and Wales is less than in other parts of continental Europe, we do consider them a significant factor in the modern Church.[163] It is difficult to consider as a generality the wide variety of groups, each of which is inspired by a specific, distinct and frequently unique vision. They are diverse in structure, ethos, degree of commitment (i.e. from a full time shared life to occasional meetings) and liturgical practice. However, we may note a number of trends: they are often lay-led, often with influences from Charismatic Renewal, their shared life is marked by being joyful and loving, they have an energy to share the Gospel which has excited them, they are often conservative in theology and moral philosophy, and they have considerable attraction to young people. These are therefore more than willing to engage in direct initial kerygmatic proclamation in many fields including street evangelisation, internet-based evangelisation, work in schools, work with youth groups, work with parishes and prayer groups, and inviting others to participate as guests in their community life. Several respondents record the influence of such movements and they seem to have a particularly significant influence on the current generation of seminarians. Not least they may challenge the parochial system with examples of vitality in Christian living.

Schools of evangelisation

These are also not yet as common in England and Wales as they seem to be elsewhere in the Catholic world. Nonetheless,

---

[163] Among these one might note the Community of St Jean {www.stjean.com}, the Emmanuel Community {www.emmanuel-info.com/en} and the Community of the Béatitudes {www.beatitudes.org}. Although these do have some English members they are very much stronger in France and elsewhere. England and Wales has some (albeit smaller) similar groups such as the Pilgrims Community {www.pilgrimscommunity.com}, Cor-Lumen Christi {www.cor-lumenchristi.org} and the Open Door Community. We should also acknowledge such movements as Cursillo, Focolare, the Neo-Catechumenate Way and several others.

initiatives have been entered into by a number of groups, and again these often are linked with Charismatic Renewal. Most take volunteers for a certain period of time and train them in particular forms of evangelising activity.

Diakonia

The proclamation and enactment of the Gospel are intimately connected: they are shoots and fruits of the same plant. Hence the ministry of service is an outworking of the Gospel and an expression of evangelisation. There is also a prophetic dimension to such service which sees the 'signs of the times' from the perspective of the Gospel and responds to those in need.

'Works of Mercy' may seem to be the language of a previous generation; there is no doubt that acts of service remain an important part of Christian discipleship. This is both in that they enact the Gospel and that they allow the Gospel to come alive in the daily lives of those disciples engaged upon them. We should remain grateful for the ongoing witness of groups such as the SVP and the Knights of St Columba and many others. Although the age profile of such groups may sometimes seem skewed to the older generations of Christians, we would wish to celebrate the work they do and their contribution to the earthing of the Gospel in practical efforts. There are several other groups which also show similar dynamics, these might include the HCPT and L'Arche communities.

Nearly a quarter of our respondents reported some voluntary 'action for justice etc. in the wider community'. The impressive array of activities included work in prisons, teaching and education, nursing and health care, credit unions, local and national politics, housing associations, supporting charities and campaign groups of many different sorts: including Amnesty International, Friends of the Earth, SPUC, Traidcraft, Christian Aid and others. Yet it is instructive to compare this impressive range of activities with the parallel fact that nearly two thirds of the same sample are involved in some Church based work. Although this core group of committed Catholics do show a laudable level of community involvement and service, the involvement in the wider community is 40 percent of the involvement in serving the inner needs of the Church.

Justice and Peace groups and campaigns have become significant parts of parish life and places where people have explored significant areas of ministry and apostolate. This has involved people in theological reflection. It has enabled people to live out, witness to and enact the Gospel in the circumstances of their lives and the context of injustice and lack of peace in the world. It has also enabled people to be deepened and renewed in their relationship to Christ and his Good News. It has also been an area where considerable empowerment of lay people has happened - not least in the harnessing of imagination in preparing campaigns, prayer and liturgy. The work of the Young Christian Workers and similar bodies have been a notable witness in this field.

Community engagement whereby the Church at the local level engages with neighbours is a powerful expression of *diakonia*. One series of examples of this are the initiatives of Broad Based Organising in which several Catholic parishes have been involved. These have been opportunities for co-operation with men and women of good will - including interfaith co-operation. They have been exercises in consultation and listening and allowing those who are often without a voice to have a voice. And they have achieved real benefits through advocacy and organisation which have caused action at local government and other levels.

Engagement with social and political processes has also been seen at the national as well as local level of government and adminstration. Certainly initiatives of the bishops have been responsible for a Catholic input based on Gospel values being heard by politicians.

The 'Integrity of Creation' has become an important theme in ecumenical missiology. We are very conscious that the Good News of Jesus is good news for all creation. Recent environmental concern and fears of ecological destruction seem to us to be places where the Gospel of Justice impels Christian action.[164]

Several of those we have talked to reported that their activities of working in this area were moments when they themselves were evangelised. Working through the inspiration of Gospel values leads to a deeper encounter with the Gospel. Seeking to enact the Gospel of Justice is not only about social transformation but leads to personal conversion and ecclesial renewal. Finding common cause with other Christians, with other people of faith, and with men and women of no explicit faith is also an opportunity to discern and discover the active grace of God in the world.

[164] See Pope John Paul II, Message for World Peace Day 1990.

8. Priorities and recommendations

Tensions and questions for discussion

Our theological enquiries, participant observations and questionnaire surveys are suggesting a number of tensions. We used these as the basis for our conversations with representatives from particular areas of interest. These we would wish to develop as ongoing areas of concern. Various of our interlocutors took what might be seen as polar positions in regard to these issues. Part of the dialectic tensions before us as a community is to maintain the mutual validity of the different emphases we have observed.

The 'conversation starters' for our discussions were as follows.

1. Ambivalence towards evangelisation
- Tendency to identify evangelisation/mission with narrow definition
- Strong positive and negative reactions to convincing others of claims of Christ
- Lack of sense of living the Christian life as bringing the Gospel into the world
- Little intuitive sense of doing things inspired by the Gospel as evangelisation (e.g. pastoral care, Justice and Peace work etc.)

Does your work make you place the emphasis on evangelisation as making new Christians or enacting the Gospel?

Would you see doing things which promote human welfare as evangelisation?

2. The move from ghetto to engagement
- Openness to world
- Reaffirming traditional strengths
- Sympathy with human person/defensiveness of institutions

Where do you feel most distinct from prevailing social trends?

Where do you feel you are most comfortable with the world outside the Church?

3. Experience

- Provision of experiences (cf. charisms) - graces from Church to world
- Listening to experiences (cf. catechumenate) - graces from world to Church
- 'Witnesses more than teachers'
- Imagination: seeing with new eyes, employing creativity

Do you feel more called to share your own experiences or build on other people's experiences?

How confident do you feel about connecting ecclesial experiences with daily life?

4. Fear and hope in the Church

- Vision
- Confident enough to criticise
- Cynicism
- Desire for security
- Living with questions not answers

What most energises you in the life of the Church?

What most drains you in the life of the Church?

5. New forms of community life beyond or semi-independent of parish

- Vitality beyond parish Mass
- Suspicion that PPs are problem (stress, overwork, depression, lack of vision, insecurity, poor standard of preaching)
- Hunger for community
- Refreshment of retreats, conferences, small groups
- Significance of schools, university chaplaincies etc., as sources of community
- Sense of irrelevance of the Church (in and beyond ecclesial community)

What are your feelings about the new forms of community / movements?

What are the strengths of parish life?

What are the weaknesses of parish life?

6. Lay formation
- Deeper evangelisation of God's people / *Mystagogia*
- Specific lay ministries
- Synthesis of faith and life
- Culture of vocation
- Teaching / learning / discovering

What would be the priorities in lay formation for you?

Where and how can lay formation best be promoted?

7. Dialogue
- Ecumenism
- Interfaith
- Culture, arts, sciences
- Modernism and Post-Modernism
- Intra-ecclesial dialogue

To what extent is dialogue part of your work?

What have you learned from dialogue?

8. Proclamation
- Direct initial kerygmatic proclamation
- 'Wordless witness'
- 'Why haven't we been taught this before?' (response to encounters with *Evangelii Nuntiandi*, Alpha, etc.)

What would you understand the *kerygma* to be?

Do you see proclamation in terms of a series of propositions or the life of a community, or as something else?

9. Service of neighbour
- Community engagement
- Justice and Peace
- Church's social teaching

Do you include community engagement or Justice and Peace work within your understanding of evangelisation?

Are our communities a place where the poor can belong?
If yes, why, and if no, why not?

10. Diversity

- No 'one size fits all'
- Need for local initiative, not just national or international statements (cf. lay apostolate)
- Mutual respect not always evident
- Flexible resourcing

Do you feel diversity is supported in the Church?

Do you feel under pressure to conform to a particular model of action?

How could an Agency for Evangelisation respond to diverse needs?

Liturgy

In some discussions the area of liturgy was raised and it was discussed whether this should be a separate category. However, reflection suggested that a liturgical focus could and should be applied to each of the above categories. Thus one may ask:

- How does liturgy express the community's understanding of evangelisation? Is the liturgy inward looking or outward looking? Is it a beacon which attracts people to the love of God? Is it Church-centred or kingdom-centred?
- Does the liturgy express Catholic identity? Is it accessible to those who are not (or not yet) Catholics? Is it inculturated? Is it faithful to Catholic tradition?
- Is it a place which offers people an experience of Good News? Is it a place where people's experiences are valued? Is it a place where people's gifts can be utilised? Without denying the centrality and necessity of the Mass are there other forms of worship which may complement it and be more accessible vehicles of evangelisation?
- Does the liturgy address fears or mask them? Is the liturgy a place of healing or a place of pain? Does the liturgy communicate hope? Does it inspire vision?

- Is the parish liturgy a place of vitality? Is the parish a 'home and school of communion'? Are there things that parochial liturgy can learn from the new forms of community and new movements?
- Is the liturgy a place of lay formation? Does it enable and foster a deeper encounter with the mystery of God's purposes? Does it work for personal development in mission and ministry? Is the liturgy a place where faith and life are synthesised?
- Is the liturgy capable of engaging with conversation with others? Is it a place where the Christian story can be told? Is it open to dialogue?
- Is the liturgy a vehicle for revealing the heart of the Gospel to those outside the Church? Do we proclaim Good News in our public worship?
- Does the liturgy equip people to serve the Church and their neighbours? Does the liturgy express the service that Christians do in the world? Is it a place where the Good News encountered in working with others can be celebrated?
- Does the liturgy protect and value diversity? Is the liturgy a place where different needs and aspirations can be expressed?

Areas for development

We would recognise a cycle of places of special significance in evangelisation.

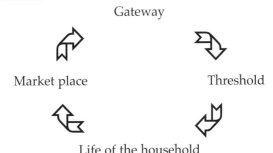

Gateway

Market place   Threshold

Life of the household

Place of evangeli-sation	Key character	Priorities of action	Examples of good practice
Gateway	Accessibility	Making contact with people, connecting with their experiences, meaning systems etc.	Alpha, 'Come and See', Seeker services
Threshold	Incorporation	Catechesis, catechumenate, journey of mutual discovery, entry into the community of faith	RCIA, Sacramental programmes
Life of household	Ecclesial renewal	Living the life of the Gospel. The Church becoming 'good news' in order to share 'good news'. Being a community which puts the Gospel into action.	Parish renewal programmes, Process based parish missions
Market place	Encounter and dialogue	Meeting with other men and women of good will. Meeting the grace of God active in the world. Being a sacrament of the kingdom in the world. Receiving 'good news' through working for Justice, Peace and Integrity of Creation.	J&P Groups, SVP, CAFOD

While all of these are happening, all could be enhanced. At the present time the most prominent of these in the life of the Church is the central strand - threshold and the life of the household. Sacramental programmes and the RCIA process are the locations where most parishes have most taken on board the demands of evangelisation. However, there is a feeling that this is often a second step, open to those who already have some contact with the Christian community and are already in a process of exploration of faith. What seems far less well developed are strategies for allowing people to make such contact with the Christian community and her life and beliefs. This involves a need for the Church to reach out to unchurched people where they are, engage with their concerns, use their language and find accessible ways of communicating the Gospel. This necessitates leaving the 'comfort zone' of ecclesial insiders in order to meet with those who are presently outside the Church.

A key condition which enables this is that the Church should be a place where people are seen to lead whole and holy lives and is perceived as a community which participates in God's purposes of love for the world. Ecclesial renewal is needed to form 'contagious Christians' whose life together expresses the authentic fullness of humanity and is attractive to others. Further, this community has a character of outreach. That is to say it looks beyond its boundaries to the world and meets people and engages with them and with issues in the world.

Key learnings

We would emphasise several key learnings.

a. The richness of scope of evangelisation
Evangelisation must be understood as a rich whole, even if particular aspects must also be emphasised. Among those aspects contributing a holistic understanding of evangelisation should be: the proclamation of the *kerygma*, conversation with and catechesis of those enquiring of the Church and seeking

possible membership, ecclesial renewal that the Church may be Good News as a condition of sharing Good News, and the commitment to enact the Gospel in the world.

Without losing the breadth we must also maintain the focus of evangelisation. It is right to see the wide compass of evangelisation and to make connections with the complex and multi-faceted truth that the establishment, communication and enacting of the Gospel brings. However, we feel it right to draw attention once more to three essential aspects of growth that lie at the heart of evangelisation: personal conversion, ecclesial renewal and social transformation. We are each called to be converted and to open ourselves personally to God in Christ; that opportunity for personal transformation in faith should be offered to all people. Catholics should not be shy of affirming our desire for every person to grow into a personal relationship with God in Christ. The Church must always be prepared herself to be renewed so that she may be a place of good news; our local communities should be places of welcome, faith and service. The Good News which transforms people and creates the Church is also to be expressed in actions which bring hope, love, justice and peace to fruition in the world; the authenticity of proclamation is to be confirmed by the reality of enacting the Gospel.

b. The orientation of Christians must be outwards

The orientation of the Church must be outward rather than inward looking. Many of our questionnaire respondents seem to paint a picture of a Church concerned with its internal self-management. While the inner health of the Church is important, and the right celebration of the sacraments of great value, these cannot lead to navel gazing. Evangelisation and mission demand that we give greater emphasis on those on and beyond our ecclesial margins - including those we may be marginalising.

The 'neighbour' is a key Gospel figure. Evangelisation must involve being good neighbours and reaching out in love to our neighbours. Christianity is not for an inner circle of believers but expresses itself in service of others. We exist for those who are not Christians. God has placed us here to do his work in his world for the neighbours he has given us in Christ. We must be with our neighbours, learn with, from and about our neighbours, relating to where their concerns are, in conversation with their langauge and thought forms and share our lives and faith with our neighbours.

The educational principle of 'starting where they are' is also the point of origin for evangelisation. People and the world are loved by God yet all too few have explicit awareness of this and cannot or do not express it in their lives. The Church must make the Good News we have received accessible to all.

c. Evangelisation is the source and fruit of communion

Communion and community life are essential to evangelisation. It is the Good News which makes us one with each other, and it is our relationships with each other which are an eloquent expression of the Gospel. The Church must become Good News in order to share Good News.[165] This calls for both the strengthening and deepening of parishes and the encouragement of small communities in which people can gather before the Word of God and share faith and life. We would note particularly the call in *Novo Millennio Ineunte* that the Church should be the 'home and school of communion'.[166] This must apply to every level of the Church's life including the domestic Church, the parish and other forms of association.

Initiatives of parish renewal have a special part to play in this. Special notice must be given to those initiatives of parish renewal which build on experiences of faith-sharing in small groups. Examples of these include the process-based parish missions of the CMS and others, RCIA, Alpha and cell groups.

The principles of unity, mutuality and relationships are at the heart of communion. The renewal of our communities to be places where people are formed in relationships of love and

[165] Mgr. David Bohr, 'Becoming and Sharing the Good News: the Nature and Content of Evangelization' in Kenneth Boyack CSP (ed.), *Catholic Evangelization Today* (Paulist Press, New York/Mahwah, 1987), p. 42.

[166] *Novo Millennio Ineunte* 43.

respect and express their individuality within corporate belonging should be a target for evangelisation. Collaboration and collaborative ministries should be considered essential expressions of this.

d. All are called to be evangelisers and formed in evangelisation

The call to evangelisation is for all Christians and therefore all should be formed in the Gospel and equipped for evangelisation. Evangelisation should clearly be part of seminary formation but it

> I am *ashamed* to say that I hold my hands up to apathy. ... Sadly none of us are drivers, we prefer to be driven.
> *Respondent to general survey*

should also be part of the equipping of every Christian. Conscious opportunities to develop in faith (such as the development of faith-sharing groups) and to actively contribute to evangelisation should be a normative part of Catholic life.

Formation is a necessary priority for the Church.[167] This is both the ongoing formation of professional workers in the Church and the universal formation of all Christians as evangelisers. The deepening of the faith and spirituality of all Christians is a pressing need. *Mystagogia* as the ongoing encounter with the mystery of faith and the development of ministries must be enhanced. This is a priority for parishes and families. This involves fostering personal, individual relationships with Christ and commitment to the corporate life of the Church as well as the witness in the world that is built on such relationships. Synthesis of faith and life as mature Christian persons represents an important goal of lay formation. Ministry for the Gospel in the world and in the Church is the consequence of such formation. An important contribution to this formation must be made by Catholic schools and educational institutions. The formation of children and young

---

[167] See Bishops' Conference Committee for Catechesis and Adult Christian Education paper, *The Priority of Adult Formation* (Catholic Media Trust, London, 2000).

adults and ministry to young families must be special moments of formation and evangelisation.

e. Conversation with the world involves both dialogue and proclamation

Dialogue and proclamation are partners in discovering, sharing and enacting the Gospel in the world. They are not opposites but complementary: both are necessary to be faithful to the Gospel. Both involve a conversation with people in the world. Both insist on making contact with those who are 'other' by finding a common language. Both are therefore essentially relational. Proclamation is about communicating to others what we have known. Dialogue is about discovering areas of common interest and understanding with others. Proclamation of the Gospel necessitates respect for those to whom we are proclaiming it. Dialogue is not about relativism but the encounter between authentic Christian belief and practice with those who are beyond explicit Christian belief and practice.

Some of the tensions which may arise between these aspects may be eased with the emphasis that what we are proclaiming is the kingdom of God. In doing so we are making contact between the experience of the Church and the experience of those beyond the Church with the aim of discovering more and sharing more about the things of God.

f. The fruit of evangelisation is service of those in need

Service of neighbour and accompanying the poorest in mission must be an articulation of evangelisation - both as a moment when the Gospel is proclaimed through its enactment and as a place where the Church is simultaneously herself evangelised and expresses her evangelisation.

Good news cannot be envisaged *in vacuo* but must be enfleshed in action. The Church must become Good News to women, men and children of today to be an authentic proclamation of the Gospel of Jesus. The authentic witness of lives lived in service to others both enables Christians to encounter the Gospel of the God of love and allows others to experience the Gospel through us.

g. Pilgrimage into God may journey down diverse roads

There are many needs and many faith journeys. To be responsive to such diversity, the Church must encourage a diverse range of initiatives in evangelisation. There is no 'one size fits all' response. Flexibility which acknowledges the distinct situations of individuals and local communities must be built in to any resourcing of evangelisation.

Evangelisation may be compared with an ecosystem within which there are several ecological niches: just as an ecosystem needs biodiversity so healthy evangelisation needs to function within a diverse series of niches. Productive growth, healthy growth and capacity to adapt to changing circumstances in ecology all need an interdependent series of relationships. So too, healthy evangelisation needs growth in mutuality, diversity and inter-dependence. Respect for diversity and protection of diversity should inform our planning for evangelisation in England and Wales.

h. Further research into specific areas of evangelisation is important

Finally, without resorting to special pleading, we would note that there is need for further and continuing research. This is for two reasons: the task of discerning the signs of times is ongoing, and also this particular piece of work is conscious of its own incompleteness. Certainly the rooting of all that we do in an understanding of where we are and where people and the world are is a journey of constant discovery. As such an attitude of openness to what is being revealed and discovered is essential. Providing information, analysis and resources that speak to the present historical and theological moment must always be a research task for the Church.

Yet in addition to this principle of openness to what may be discovered, the authors of this particular work feel obliged to admit our limitations. In this report there have been several areas we have scarcely touched upon but which merit deeper attention. These include:

- Evangelisation and the work of Catholic schools.
- Collaborative ministry and evangelisation.

- Seminary formation and evangelisation.
- Appropriate training for and formation in evangelisation for all Christians.
- The spirituality, faith and values of the those who have left the Church.
- Comparison between fringe members of the Church to the Core of Church membership.
- The spirituality, faith and values of the unchurched.
- Ecumenism, interfaith dialogue and evangelisation.
- The development of 'Emerging Church' and experiments in Post-Evangelical and alternative worship movements and how these may impact Catholic spirituality and practice.
- Appropriate forms of worship and evangelisation.
- More detailed analysis of specific locations of evangelisation and models of evangelisation touched on here such as the New Movements and Communities, parish and school mission processes, forms of initial kerygmatic proclamation and initiatives of service.

Appendix. Notes on Surveys - Participation and Sample Size

A major instrument of the research outlined in this report was a series of questionnaires directed at several constituencies. There were four target populations to which questionnaires were distributed, namely:

- the general parish population,
- parish priests,
- bishops, diocesan officers and other non-parochial workers,
- seminary students.

The questionnaires were designed to be descriptive in nature with the aim of gathering information about people's experiences and perceptions of evangelisation. The size of the target population for each survey ranged from 96 to in excess of 4 million. The largest target population for the surveys was the number of people in England and Wales that could be estimated to belong to a Catholic parish. There is no simple formula for determining an adequate sample size for such a large and potentially diverse population. General guiding principles suggest that small samples are more likely to introduce error and bias than large ones. In other words, a large sample is to be preferred.

For descriptive surveys, such as opinion polls and market research based on very large target populations a sample size of 1,000 is generally considered to produce a good representation of the 'true' population. Hence, it was considered desirable to achieve a response from upwards of 1,000 parishioners in order to produce a sample that was likely to be representative of the general parish population.

Regardless of the number of people surveyed it is the case that in any survey there will always be a certain degree of variation within the individual members of the target population. Hence, in addition to sample size it was also important to consider an appropriate sampling technique that would minimise the likelihood of bias and that would allow any member of the target population an equal chance of being selected. Accordingly, a random sampling technique was employed since this is the method to be preferred in order to reduce bias and produce a sample that most accurately reflects the characteristics of the 'true' population.

In order to achieve the desired response rate of 1,000 parishioners 5,000 questionnaires were distributed in 1,250 randomly chosen Catholic parishes in England and Wales. Equally, a random sample of 1,250 parish priests (in the same parishes) was also selected and requested to complete a separate questionnaire.

In addition, 120 questionnaires were randomly distributed to bishops, diocesan officers and other non-parochial workers and the entire population of seminary students was sent a postal survey. Response rates to the surveys for each of the target populations is outlined below:

Target Population	% Response to survey
Parishioners	23
Parish priests	36
Bishops/diocesan officers	55
Seminary students	44

Notes of caution

Whilst the sample for each constituency surveyed was as representative as was feasible within the budget and time scale of the research remit we are aware that the responses are likely to contain some elements of bias. For instance, there is no simple way of distributing 5,000 surveys to parishioners from a largely inaccessible sampling frame. The reason being that the priest in charge of the parish was requested to select these individuals, albeit according to carefully structured guidelines as to how the surveys should be distributed in order to avoid bias. It is possible that some priests did not adhere to the guidelines, perhaps due to difficulties in achieving responses from some individuals or due to lack of access to, or an incomplete knowledge of, certain elements of the parish population. Hence, it is possible that the sample of parishioners is in reality inclined to be more subjective.

In contrast, we can be sure that the responses from parish priests represent an accurate random sample and we can therefore be confident of the precision of the sample in terms of representing the 'true' population for this constituency. The sample of parish priests also represents more than 10 percent of the total number of secular clergy in England and Wales, which is a more than satisfactory response.

Overall, the findings from the four surveys bear comparison with the results from other recent surveys related to aspects of mission and evangelisation. Most notably, the results of the Church Life Profile (CLP),[168] conducted in April 2001, tend to validate the accuracy of many of the findings resulting from the survey of parishioners and uphold the ascertain that the responses are drawn from a representative sample. There is much similarity between the two surveys in relation to some of the key characteristics of the general parish population. Most notably with regard to the general structure of the parish population, measures of parish vitality, involvement in social action and in appreciation of what the CLP terms 'valued aspects of church' such as liturgy, preaching and pastoral care.

The accuracy with which the results from the survey strand of this research can be interpreted are fundamentally dependent on the variation between individuals in each of the survey samples and on the sample size. We have attempted to reduce variation as much as possible within the limits of the research remit by the choice of sampling method and large sample size. The questionnaires provide a reliable, unique and valid description of people's experience and understanding of evangelisation in the Catholic Church in England and Wales.

[168] The Church Life Profile is part of the International Congregational Life Survey (ICLS), conducted in England by Churches Information for Mission {www.cim.org.uk}. The results will provide individualised mission resources for participating churches (at the level of the local parish or equivalent). It is one of the largest surveys ever undertaken in Britain with 100,000 participants.

The original surveys are available at {www.cms.org.uk/research} as are the graphical results for each question from every constituency.

The Search for Christian Unity

The Search for Christian Unity - approved by the Bishops' Conference of England and Wales - is a popular version of the Vatican's *Directory for the Application of Principles and Norms on Ecumenism*.

Chapter 1, 'The search for Christian unity', makes the Catholic Church's ecumenical commitment very clear.

Chapter 2, 'Organisation in the Catholic Church at the service of Christian unity', describes how the Church officially structures its search for unity.

Chapter 3, 'Ecumenical formation in the Catholic Church', deals with the vital issue of learning about ecumenism and forming an ecumenical attitude.

Chapter 4, 'Communion in life and spiritual activity among the baptised', spells out appropriate ways of sharing in prayer and in both sacramental and non-sacramental worship.

Chapter 5, 'Ecumenical co-operation, dialogue and common witness', looks at practical details of working, witnessing and sharing in dialogue together.

The Search for Christian Unity includes study questions and points for action, and a foreword by Cardinal Cormac Murphy-O'Connor.

The Search for Christian Unity, A5, 80 pages, £4.00, ISBN 0 905241 21 5.

Teachers of the Faith:
speeches and lectures by Catholic bishops

Six cardinals and three other bishops have contributed to a unique collection of speeches and lectures, entitled *Teachers of the Faith*. All of the lectures were delivered in Britain over the last 26 years, and have appeared in the pages of *Briefing*, the official monthly journal of the Catholic bishops of Britain.

- **Cardinal Basil Hume** speaks about his personal faith journey and Jesus Christ today.
- **Cardinal Thomas Winning** discusses the Church in the third millennium.
- **Cardinal Cahal Daly**'s two contributions concern Northern Ireland, and the moral challenges facing the Church.
- **Cardinal Joseph Ratzinger**'s address is on consumer materialism and Christian hope.
- **Cardinal Johannes Willebrands** asks, is Christianity anti-Semitic?
- **Archbishop Derek Worlock** reflects on Catholic education and the 1944 Education Act.
- **Bishop Alan Clark** discusses the movement to Christian unity.
- **Bishop James Sangu** of Tanzania examines justice in the African context.

The foreword is by Cardinal Cormac Murphy-O'Connor.

Teachers of the Faith: speeches and lectures by Catholic bishops, A5, 160 pages, £6.00, ISBN 0 905241 19 3

Interfaith Dialogue -
the teaching of the Catholic Church

The Catholic bishops of England and Wales have published a major new resource on interreligious dialogue. This new book presents the Church's teaching on other religions and on relations with people of other faiths.

Compiled by the bishops' Committee for Other Faiths, it brings together important extracts from official Church documents from the Second Vatican Council decrees to the interreligious meeting this year in Assisi.

Chapters cover the Church's basic teaching on interfaith dialogue, and specific sections on Judaism, Islam and other faiths.

This book is a useful resource and reference work for Catholics and non-Catholics alike seeking to further understand the Church's approach to dialogue.

Interfaith Dialogue - the teaching of the Catholic Church, A5, 64 pages, £3.00, ISBN: 0 905241 22 3

Briefing

Briefing is the official monthly journal of the Catholic Bishops' Conferences of Great Britain. It contains documents, information and news from the Church in Britain, Rome and overseas; official documents from the official sources.

£29.50 annual subscription.

Catholic Communications Service, 39 Eccleston Square, London SW1V 1BX